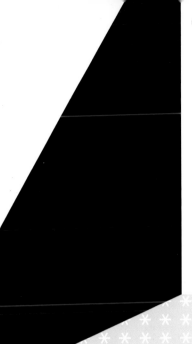

The Information Design Handbook

Jenn + Ken Visocky O'Grady

1

A Need for Information Design

2

Information Design Defined

3

ID History: Innovation & Impact

4

Cognitive Principles for ID

5

Communication Principles for ID

6

Aesthetic Principles for ID

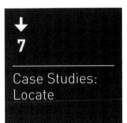

7

Case Studies: Locate

8

Case Studies: Perform

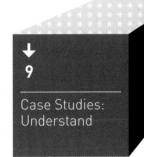

9

Case Studies: Understand

RotoVision

Section 1

Overview

6

1

A Need for Information Design

8

9   Globalization Through Technology

12 Spending More Time at Work

14 More Media, More Messages

16 The Value of Design

2

Information Design Defined

17

18 The Designer's Perspective

23 Common Information Design Artifacts

25 User-Centered Design

26 ISO 13407: Human-Centered Design Model

3

ID History: Innovation & Impact

27

28 Cave Paintings and Petroglyphs

29 Pictographic Writing

30 Early Cartography

33 Charts and Graphs

34 ISOTYPE

38 Guides for Structuring Information

40 The Interactive Exhibit

44 The *Pioneer* Plaque

46 The Visible Language Workshop

50 The First Website

Section 2

Principles

52

4

Cognitive Principles for ID

54

55 Learning Styles

58 Cognitive Processes

58 *Memory*

62 *Perception and Discernment*

72 *Wayfinding*

75 *Information Overload*

5

Communication Principles for ID

78

80 Organization

80 *AIDA*

82 *LATCH*

84 *Inverted Pyramid Writing*

86 Familiarity

86 *Principle of Least Effort*

88 *Uncertainty Reduction Theory*

91 Literacy

Section 3

Case Studies

132

6

Aesthetic
Principles
for ID

96

98 Structure

98 *Grid Systems*

105 *Hierarchy*

108 Legibility

108 *Color*

116 *Contrast*

120 *Typography*

7

Case Studies:
Locate

134

135 Adams +
Associates
Design
Consultants,
Inc.

138 Justice Mapping
Center (JMC) &
Spatial Information
Design Lab (SIDL)
at Columbia
University

142 Kick Design, Inc.

144 Los Angeles
County
Metropolitan
Transportation
Authority (Metro)

146 Pentagram Design

149 Sussman/Prejza
& Co., Inc.

8

Case Studies:
Perform

151

152 AdamsMorioka

154 Meeker &
Associates and
Terminal Design

156 Pentagram Design

158 Read Regular

160 Satellite Design

162 Scheme, LTD.

164 Studio Panepinto,
LLC

166 Ultimate Symbol

9

Case Studies:
Understand

169

170 C&G Partners

172 Chopping Block

174 Design Council

176 Drake Exhibits

178 Explanation
Graphics

180 Explanation
Graphics

181 Futurefarmers

184 Inaria Brand
Design Consultants

186 Jazz at Lincoln
Center In-house
Design

188 Andreas Koller and
Philipp Steinweber

192 LA ink

194 Nobel Web

197 Number 27

201 Sooy & Co.

203 TesisDG

205 White Rhino

208 Glossary

214 Contributors

218 Resources

219 References

220 Bibliography

221 Index

224 Thanks

224 About the Authors

Overview

In a complex world, clear and accessible communication, across a broad range of media, has become essential. Information design addresses this need by blending typography, illustration, communication studies, ergonomics, psychology, sociology, linguistics, computer science, and a variety of other fields to create concise and unambiguous messages. While virtually all forms of design are human-centered, information design focuses on the accurate representation of specific knowledge sets and the unique needs of the end user receiving that content.

This section provides an overview of the increasing relevance of information design, explores its classification by practitioners and industry leaders, reviews the artifacts most commonly associated with the delivery of its messages, and provides a historical context for the emergence of this practice as a profession.

The demand for universally accessible knowledge is increasing in step with the pace of the modern world.

In an age of information and global connectivity, governments, corporations, educational institutions, and individuals alike struggle to find better ways to communicate.

Geographic, cultural, and language barriers, combined with a glut of conflicting messages, available media channels, and consumer choices, have created an overwhelming need for clarity, of which the information designer is champion.

Consider the following trends and their implications for designers:

Trend: Globalization Through Technology
Advances in technology and communication are driving phenomenal change. Consider the computer and the internet, the former developed for military applications, and the latter (in its ARPANET origins[1]) to connect a handful of universities and governmental agencies. When the first four computers were connected in 1969, no one could have guessed the impact on the world citizen four decades later. Current estimates place today's average internet user online for approximately 31 hours per month.[2] Each of those users has the power to access or distribute a vast amount of information from anywhere in the world with an internet connection.

Research on worldwide internet usage indicates that Asia, North America, and Europe comprise the majority of online users, but usage in the Middle East, Latin America, and Africa has grown by more than 400% over the last several years. Usage worldwide has increased by 225% since 2000, and many nonprofit organizations and companies are working to rapidly improve the rate of inclusion.

English and Chinese are the top two languages represented on the internet, each with approximately 30% of users. The languages rounding out the top 10 are Spanish, Japanese, German, French, Portuguese, Korean, Italian, and Arabic.[3] With communication technology spreading rapidly, clear visual (and sometimes nonverbal) communication is of paramount importance when sharing ideas and concepts with a broad audience.

1. The ARPANET (Advanced Research Projects Agency Network) was the first attempt at sharing information between computers using existing telephone lines. For a more in-depth discussion of the ARPANET and the history of the internet, visit the Computer History Museum in Mountain View, California, USA. Or go online to http://www.computerhistory.org/internet_history

2. Usage time statistic provided by a 2006 Comscore study; specifics at http://www.comscore.com/press/release.asp?press=849

3. For more statistical information on internet usage worldwide, go to http://internetworldstats.com

A network diagram of the original four computers and their respective universities connected by the ARPANET in 1969.

From Left:

*Honeywell DDP-516 computer
University of California
Los Angeles*

*IBM 360/75 computer
University of California
Santa Barbara*

*SDS-940 computer
Stanford Research Institute*

*DEC PDP-10 computer
University of Utah*

1	2	3	4
Honeywell DDP-516	IBM 360/75	SDS-940	DEC PDP-10
UCLA	**UCSB**	**SRI**	**Utah**

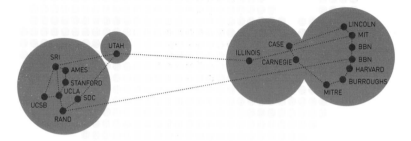

This diagram shows the rapid expansion of the ARPANET in 1971 as more research institutions came online.

An IBM 360/75 computer, like the machines pictured here, was one of the first units connected to the ARPANET. Note that what you might consider the "computer" by today's standards is, in this case, only the terminal. The actual processor is the large, cabinet-like structure.

Design Implications:
World Smaller, Client Base Larger

Communication technology allows people to globally share information that was once targeted at local or very specific end users. From news and entertainment to proprietary information about goods and services, designers now must communicate ideas to people who may or may not share their native language, aesthetic sensibilities, or cultural understanding. As internet usage increases and more and more societies are represented online, communication efforts must be able to cross language and cultural barriers. Clear visual representation of information is imperative for the comprehension of existing knowledge, the creation of new knowledge, the expansion of economies, and ultimately our understanding of one another.

1. Source for graphs: internetworldstats.com

Internet Usage by World Region

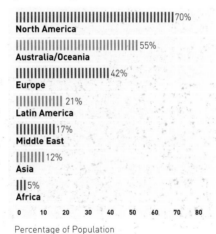

Asia	459M
Europe	338M
North America	235M
Latin America	116M
Africa	44M
Middle East	34M
Australia/Oceania	19M

0 50 100 150 200 250 300 350 400 450 500

Millions of Users

Internet Penetration by World Region

North America	70%
Australia/Oceania	55%
Europe	42%
Latin America	21%
Middle East	17%
Asia	12%
Africa	5%

0 10 20 30 40 50 60 70 80

Percentage of Population

Top Seven Languages on the Internet

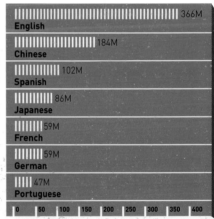

English	366M
Chinese	184M
Spanish	102M
Japanese	86M
French	59M
German	59M
Portuguese	47M

0 50 100 150 200 250 300 350 400

Millions of Users

↑ ↗
While Asia has the largest number of users online, it also has one of the lowest penetration rates, indicating the potential for growth in this region as technology and internet access become more readily available.[1]

→
Even though Asia has the largest number of internet users, English remains the dominant language.

1. From "One Day in America— America by the Numbers," time.com, http://www.time.com/time/specials/2007/article/0,28804,1674995_1683300,00.html

2. From a Statistics Canada study, popularly disseminated by the Canadian Broadcast Corporation. A news release is available at http://www.cbc.ca/canada/story/2007/02/13/family-time.html

3. This information is from a Sleep Council press release, available at http://www.sleepcouncil.com

4. Graph created with data from the Organisation for Economic Co-operation and Development's (OECD) "Employment Outlook: 2003 Statistical Annex." This visualization is meant to provide a generalization of workforce trends (as part- and full-time workers are counted equally). The document is available for download at http://www.oecd.org

Trend: Spending More Time at Work

As technological progress marches ever onward, so too does the amount of time we spend working each day. As individuals try to keep pace with the 24/7 reality of the global economy, many countries report that their citizens are spending more time at work and that mobile devices and e-mail have invaded leisure and family time. According to an article published in *Time* magazine in 2007, "Modern parents multitask about 40 more hours a week than did their counterparts in 1975."[1] In Canada, longer working days have cut into personal time by 45 minutes per day (a total of 195 hours per year).[2] And the United Kingdom's Sleep Council cites "the demands of commerce and industry, the sheer speed of international communications, and globalization of the marketplace" as disruptive to sleep patterns.[3]

While the hours spent at work are generally on the rise, individuals still find time to do the things that they enjoy, and to engage with family and friends. This means that we're all "multitasking" more than ever before.

Design Implications: Divided Focus

Designers must have an increased awareness of the pressures and time constraints placed on their audience. Information sets should be easy to absorb as well as efficient in delivery. Think about the modern airport patron as an example. Most are conversing wirelessly or text messaging while navigating the terminal. Because their attention is more inwardly focused than ever before, subtle signage has less impact. When signage is unclear, patrons bump into each other, spend more time asking for assistance, and risk missed connections. Information design systems need to be transparent in their message (users doesn't want to think, they just want to understand). They also need to be adaptive to the kinetic needs of the user. The need for clarity and the accelerated pace of modern living make the information designer's skills increasingly valuable.

→ *Across the globe, we are spending more time at work. This diagram shows national averages for hours worked, per person, in a given year.*[4]

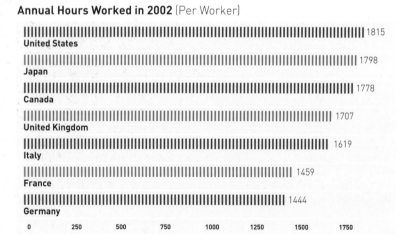

Annual Hours Worked in 2002 (Per Worker)

United States 1815
Japan 1798
Canada 1778
United Kingdom 1707
Italy 1619
France 1459
Germany 1444

0   250   500   750   1000   1250   1500   1750

Because of their newfound connectivity with employers, contemporary workers often incorporate work duties into other facets of their lives. Compounded by the demands of family, friends, and daily life, our attention is certainly divided.

Trend: More Media, More Messages

For most of human history, information has been communicated at a relatively slow pace. Before the advent of commercial printing, information was spread verbally; books were rare, expensive, and created by hand, and literacy levels were low. The advent of movable type and printing presses dramatically increased the distribution of content, followed eventually by the invention of mass-media outlets such as radio and television. The second half of the twentieth century offered a media-rich environment, but one primarily based on sender–receiver models. Compare that to the world in which we now live. Your day may include messages delivered via print, television, radio, website, e-mail, text message, podcast, webcast, blog, social network, guerilla or viral marketing, interactive outdoor advertising—even spam! And those are just a few of the media channels competing for your attention. Measure this change (much of it occurring over the course of a mere decade) not only by the sheer number of communication vehicles, but by the paradigm shift that allows the consumers of messages to become creators, too. Discourse is now projected in real time, with none of the information lag of traditional media.

Design Implications: More to Learn, More to Offer

Technology and communication have always been inextricably linked, and exponential growth in one leads to increased production of the other. There has never been more content to sift through, or so many ways to access it. With so much new material being generated each day there are unprecedented needs and opportunities for designers to create meaningful contexts.

Historically, designers have responded to technological changes by updating their tools—moving from ruling pens to Rapidographs to Adobe Illustrator. With this focus on deadlines and production, the cultural shifts associated with new media may be overlooked. The communication paradigms of users evolve as quickly as the tools themselves; thus, it is imperative to comprehend preferred methods of media consumption (print, web, mobile device), and to understand how and why audiences are using those tools. This human-centered approach to design positions today's practitioner as a valued communication consultant, rather than a service provider billing per artifact.

→

Historically, information has been distributed through a variety of centralized networks. First, handwritten documents were authored by an individual and passed to specific users. With the advent of printing, documents could be produced more quickly, but they remained rare and literacy rates were low. Mass-media outlets such as newspapers, radio, and television provided the means of distribution to a much larger audience, but content was still primarily sent from a centralized source. The internet has created an entirely new information delivery paradigm in which users can communicate directly with multiple information sources—and with each other—all in real time, creating a distributive network.

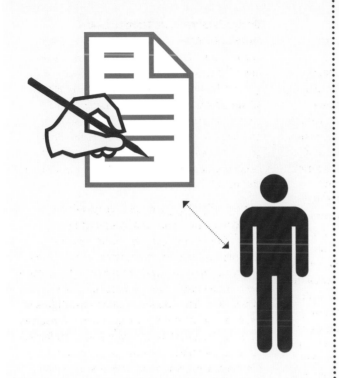

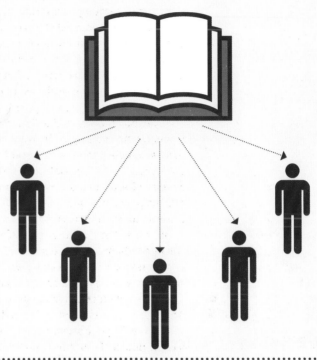

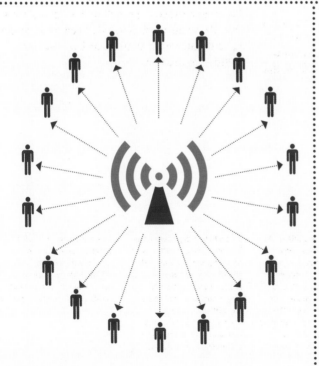

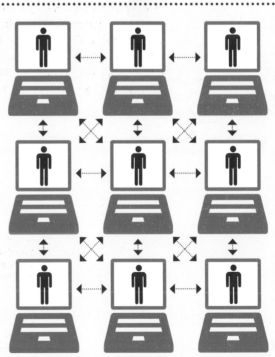

1. This study was undertaken by University of California Berkeley's School of Information Management and Systems. Results are available online at http://www2.sims.berkeley.edu/research/projects/how-much-info-2003/execsum.htm

The Value of Design

The world's store of information is growing exponentially. A recent study estimates the amount of new knowledge created and stored in 2002 to be five exabytes—37,000 times the total amount of information stored in books at the United States Library of Congress. That number had doubled from a similar study completed just two years before.[1] Consider, though, that information delivery is dependent on clarity of communication to retain its relevance to a global audience. Designers provide that context by turning statistics into stories, providing meaning for the end user. As our world becomes more complex, this expertise is increasingly important to the ways in which we live, work, and share ideas.

→

Information volume is difficult to visualize. This illustration provides context for the standards of measurement used to describe digital information stores.

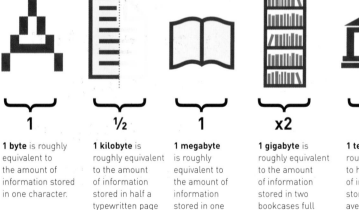
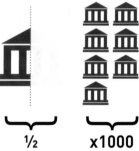

1	½	1	x2	½	x1000
1 byte is roughly equivalent to the amount of information stored in one character.	**1 kilobyte** is roughly equivalent to the amount of information stored in half a typewritten page	**1 megabyte** is roughly equivalent to the amount of information stored in one small novel.	**1 gigabyte** is roughly equivalent to the amount of information stored in two bookcases full of books.	**1 terabyte** is roughly equivalent to half the amount of information stored in the average academic research library.	**1 exabyte** is roughly equivalent to 7,000 times the amount of information in print at the US Library of Congress.

Finding a single, comprehensive definition for the term "information design" is almost impossible. It's better to explore the discipline through the words of its most noted practitioners, review the artifacts commonly associated with the visualization of data, and investigate the philosophy of a user-centered approach.

The Designer's Perspective

We each have a different perspective on the information we receive—this is apparent when traveling companions consult a map in a foreign city, when coworkers deliberate over the instruction manual for a broken copier, or when children review the rules of a game.

And who are the brave folks who dare to present these documents to the masses? That's right, designers. More specifically, information designers.

The following quotes were collected from books, printed or digital articles, and websites. They represent discourse on the discipline by its most seasoned practitioners and are a fitting introduction to a chapter dedicated to shedding light on the term "information design." Enjoy the cacophony of opinion. Note where it converges and diverges. Borrow as appropriate.

> "Information design makes complex information easier to understand and to use."
>
> —*AIGA*
> from aiga.org

> "Information design is about the clear and effective presentation of information. It involves a multi- and interdisciplinary approach to communication, combining skills from graphic design, technical and non-technical authoring, psychology, communication theory, and cultural studies."
>
> —*Frank Thissen*
> translated from *Lexikon des Digitalen Informations Designs*

"Information design is all about the psychology and physiology of how users access, learn, and remember information; the impact of colors, shapes, and patterns, learning styles."

—*Luigi Canali De Rossi*
from "What is Information Design?" at masterviews.com

"My quote is: 'The only way to communicate is to understand what it is like not to understand.' It is at that moment that you can make something understandable."

—*Richard Saul Wurman*
from "The InfoDesign Interview" at informationdesign.org

"Information design addresses the organization and presentation of data: its transformation into valuable, meaningful information."

—*Nathan Shedroff*
from nathan.com

"Information design is defined as the art and science of preparing information so that it can be used by human beings with efficiency and effectiveness. Information design's primary products appear as documents and as presentations on computer screens."

—*Robert E. Horn*
from *Information Design*

"Information design is the defining, planning, and shaping of the contents of a message and the environments it is presented in with the intention of achieving particular objectives in relation to the needs of users."

—*International Institute for Information Design*
from iiid.net

"Information design is the transfer of complex data to, for the most part, two-dimensional visual representations that aim at communicating, documenting, and preserving knowledge. It deals with making entire sets of facts and their interrelations comprehensible, with the objective of creating transparency and eliminating uncertainty."

—*Gerlinde Schuller*
from "Information Design = Complexity + Interdisciplinarity + Experiment" at aiga.org

"**Information designers are very special people who must master all of the skills and talents of a designer; combine them with the rigor and problem-solving ability of a scientist or mathematician; and bring the curiosity, research skills, and doggedness of a scholar to their work.**"

—*Terry Irwin*
from "Information Design: What is it and Who does it?" at aiga.org

"Information design, also known as communication design, is a rapidly growing discipline that draws on typography, graphic design, applied linguistics, applied psychology, applied ergonomics, computing, and other fields. It emerged as a response to people's need to understand and use such things as forms, legal documents, signs, computer interfaces, technical information, and operating/assembly instructions."

—*Sue Walker and Mark Barratt*
for Design Council, from designcouncil.org.uk

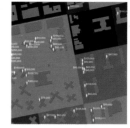

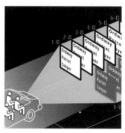

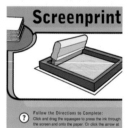

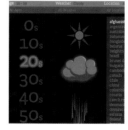

Common Information Design Artifacts
We are all inundated with media choices.

Likewise, there are numerous strategies that the information designer can employ to deliver a particular message. The artifacts most commonly associated with information design serve a range of functions. Some are pure visualizations of data, helping to clarify or summarize complex content and large quantities of information (charts in an annual report/demonstrative evidence/a medical illustration). Others deliver immediate nonverbal messages (the women's lavatory is here/caution, steep descent ahead/don't consume, this is poison). Some simplify complex concepts, others provide context, and the most ingenious help to visualize entirely new connections.

The function (and often the physical form) of the design piece is primarily determined by two factors: the information density, and the audience. Imagine the different communication paradigms involved in a project for a large, international, multilingual audience, and those for an limited, industry-specific job. Similarly, the quantity and accessibility of the content affects the suitability of a specific vehicle. Consider the information density of a business card versus that of a company directory. Who is the intended recipient of each artifact?

The following artifacts are utilized by information designers according to the needs of the end user, the resources of the client, and the time available.

· *Calendars, timelines, and timetables*

· *Charts and graphs*

· *Diagrams and schematics*

· *Exhibitions and environments*

· *Exterior signage, wayfinding elements, and kiosks*

· *Icons and symbols*

· *Interfaces, both physical and digital*

· *Maps*

· *3-D models and computer simulations*

· *Storyboards and narratives*

· *Technical illustrations*

· *Tutorials and instructions*

· *Websites, animations, and interactive media*

←

Information designers understand which artifacts and communication channels will relay their message most effectively.

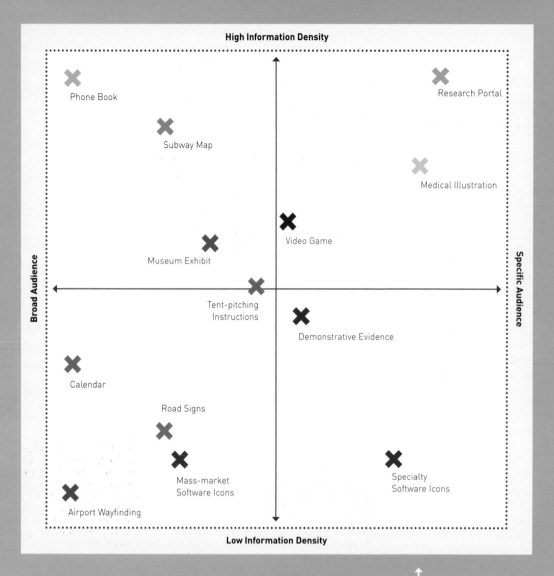

High Information Density

Phone Book

Research Portal

Subway Map

Medical Illustration

Video Game

Broad Audience

Museum Exhibit

Specific Audience

Tent-pitching
Instructions

Demonstrative Evidence

Calendar

Road Signs

Mass-market
Software Icons

Specialty
Software Icons

Airport Wayfinding

Low Information Density

↑
The form and function of information design artifacts are determined by two factors: the knowledge base of the audience, and information density. This chart shows where various design artifacts fall in that equation. For example, a medical illustration of the *skeleton would be targeted at a very specific audience, and packed with detailed information. Conversely, road signage is targeted at a much broader audience, and its messages are concise.*

User-centered Design

User-centered design, or human-centered design, places the end user at the center of the design process.

Often associated with human–computer interaction and ergonomics, this philosophy can also be used in the development of artifacts that are interactive, print-based, or three-dimensional.

User-centered design is driven by research. Research during the developmental process provides valuable insight into the needs, behaviors, and expectations of the target audience. Focus groups, interviews, ethnographic and observational studies, and other tactics help the designer to create the most effective communication piece. Emphasis is placed on iteration and participation. Projects are developed through cycles of testing, analysis, and refinement. Multiple iterations often provoke questions and solutions previously unforeseen by the design team. Engaging a sample of actual end users to participate in the vetting process guides a project toward further refinement. The goal is to create artifacts that enhance the way people work, learn, and play—rather than forcing them to conform to new or unfamiliar skill sets and learning methods.

Information design is ultimately a human-centered practice. Careful consideration of the user's needs determines the appropriate content.

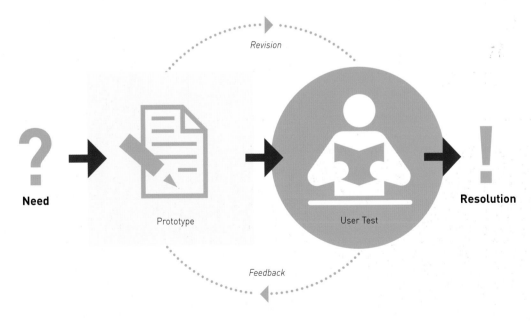

Need

Prototype

Revision

User Test

Feedback

Resolution

An iterative process employs several cycles of prototyping and testing to determine the best possible solution to a design problem. Engaging end users in the testing stages ensures a product that will meet the needs of its audience.

ISO 13407: Human-Centered Design Model

There are many process models for user-centered design, but they all share common themes.

Whether touted by professional organizations as an example of best practice, or proprietary to a specific studio, each begins by defining the problem; moves through research, prototyping, testing, and refinement; and then focuses on delivery. One model to note is available through the International Organization for Standardization (ISO), a global consortium of standard-setting bodies. In 1999, the ISO published its own human-centered design model, ISO 13407. This international standard for a user-centered approach to project development divides the design process into four stages:

· Specify the context of use

· Specify the user and organizational requirements

· Produce design solutions

· Evaluate designs against project requirements

While specifically aimed at interactive products, the process described in ISO 13407 can be applied to any design problem. It may be similar to the proprietary model your firm uses, but ISO 13407 is an internationally recognized standard of practice. ISO standards are documented international agreements that contain detailed information regarding technology and business practices. They are used as guidelines that assure the quality of products and services, and are a recognized benchmark of quality around the globe. The International Organization for Standardization represents 157 nations, and the standards that it prescribes often become part of trade agreements and treaties. A powerful business tool, ISO practices can help the designer assure the client of quality while ensuring that the project meets its intended goals. For further information on ISO 13407, go to http://www.iso.org.

The human-centered design model described by ISO 13407 is an iterative process that tests design prototypes against predetermined user needs. These tests can be undertaken with either real or fictitious users. ISO 13407 was created for interactive products, but can be effectively applied to any design project.

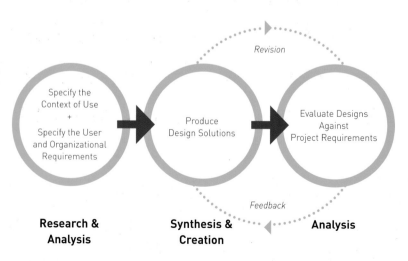

A truly detailed history of information design would take years to compile, several volumes to house, and a long time to read. This chapter is instead meant as an overview, exploring some key innovations in communication and discussing their impact on society and the practice of design. To forecast the future, it is important to have an understanding of the past.

Innovation: Cave Paintings and Petroglyphs

Images were used as a means of communication 30,000 years before early writing first appeared in Mesopotamia (circa 3000 BCE).

1. The empiricist theory was the most widely accepted explanation of cave art until trance theory was postulated.

2. For more about David Lewis-Williams's trance theory, see *The Mind in the Cave: Consciousness and the Origins of Art* (Thames & Hudson, 2004).

These prehistoric markings can be found all over the globe in the form of cave paintings, cliff drawings, and petroglyphs (pictures, symbols, or other imagery carved into natural rock surfaces), and represent the first known attempt at the visual representation of information. Famous cave painting sites include the Altamira cave in Spain, and Lascaux and Chauvet in France. The Chauvet cave is considered by many scholars to be the site of the world's oldest cave paintings, containing imagery over 30,000 years old. These Paleolithic rock galleries depict 13 different species of animals—primarily hunt animals such as deer and cattle, but also rarely seen images of predators including lions, hyenas, and bears.

Opinions differ regarding the symbolism of early cave painting, but two dominant concepts are the empiricist and trance theories. The empiricist approach considers mankind's early markings to be motivated by a need to record important events in the life of the individual and the community, as well as to educate the young and provide a cathartic means of self-expression.[1] Trance theory, born from ethnographic studies of contemporary hunter-gatherer cultures, argues that cave paintings were created by shamans, members of the community who attained altered states of consciousness and created images in an effort to contact spirits, control the lives of animals, change the weather, and heal the sick.[2]

Impact

Cave paintings and petroglyphs are the first examples we have of visual communication. It is difficult, in our visually dominated culture, to comprehend the importance of those first markings. Visual records, whether made for practical or spiritual purposes, transformed the way humans shared ideas, beliefs, and experiences.

→
Petroglyphs are symbols carved directly into rock. Examples are scattered across the globe, rendered by numerous cultures with varied intent. These are by the Ancestral Puebloans, who populated the American West.

Innovation: Pictographic Writing

Humans had been creating visual imagery for several thousand years, but the first writing as we would recognize it was not developed until 3000 BCE in Sumer, a region of Mesopotamia that is often called "the cradle of civilization."

Developed as a means of accounting, the Sumerian pictographic writing system was imprinted on clay tokens used for commerce. Those tokens were stored in sealed jars, which were imprinted with the quantities they contained. Later, clay tablets were used to keep records of agricultural and trade goods.

Original Sumerian writing read from top to bottom with the pictographs oriented along a horizon line (similar to "stacked" type). Over time, the figures rotated and became more abstract and wedge-shaped, leading to what we now recognize as cuneiform script. As the writing evolved, marks began to represent phonetic sounds, in addition to their pictographic symbolism. A similar phenomenon was concurrent in China and Egypt. Eventually, phonetic representation became the dominant form.

Impact

Like image- and mark-making, writing is a skill that modern humans take for granted. While imagery is certainly an important tool for communication, writing provides a more precise means to share and distribute ideas among a large population. Writings enables us to record history, exchange information beyond geographic boundaries, communicate knowledge to future generations, and build upon the ideas of the past.

	Sag **Head**	Gin **To Walk**	Šu **Hand**	Še **Barley**	Ninda **Bread**	A **Water**	Ud **Day**	Mušen **Bird**

This chart illustrates the evolution of early Sumerian writing. The pictographic symbols rotate and eventually become abstracted, with repeated common strokes.

Innovation: Early Cartography

Cartography, the art and science of creating maps, can also trace its history back to preliterate man: maps are one of the earliest forms of information design.

References to celestial bodies have been found in cave paintings around the world. Historians, however, are unsure of their use. Were they directional, descriptive, or possibly used for ritual worship? Ethnographic research among contemporary hunter-gatherer societies indicates that early humans would have had a highly developed sense of direction, relied primarily on memorization for survival, and would not have traveled vast distances to hunt their prey—so they wouldn't have needed maps for geographic wayfinding.

There is plenty of academic contention regarding what should be considered the first map, but the Town Plan of Nippur is certainly one of the earliest cartographic documents. Inscribed into clay in Sumer circa 1300 BCE, it depicts the layout of a town, indicating waterways and the locations of man-made structures with notations in cuneiform.

Believed to be instrumental in fortifying defenses and rebuilding the town, the Town Plan of Nippur is also of historical significance because it is the first known example to combine several key factors of mapmaking: orientation, notation, and scale.

Impact

As humans made the transition from hunter-gatherer to agrarian societies and began to develop more sophisticated technology, maps became more complex. In 150 CE, Ptolemy wrote the *Geographia*, a document that contained detailed accounts of the world's geography in the second century. The Romans created accurate maps of newly conquered lands to manage the construction of roads and property rights for their vast empire. Renaissance cartographers created highly detailed charts depicting coastlines, ports, geographic hazards, and wind directions. Advances in measurement and production technology led to more detailed maps with denser information resolution and greater representational accuracy. Today, highly accurate satellite imagery is available to any internet user via tools like Google Earth™ and National Geographic's MapMachine. Satellite navigation systems are available on any web-connected device and even in automobiles and mobile phones.

The Town Plan of Nippur is considered by many to be the first example of modern cartography. Created in Sumer (near modern-day Baghdad) circa 1300 BCE, it utilizes orientation, notation, and scale in its

depiction of the town of Nippur. Historians suggest that this map was used as a reference for fortifying defenses and rebuilding.

Ptolemy's Geographia was an ambitious and detailed attempt to document the world's geography during the second century CE. New editions of Ptolemy's maps, or those heavily influenced by Geographia,

were produced well into the Renaissance and beyond (as shown here).

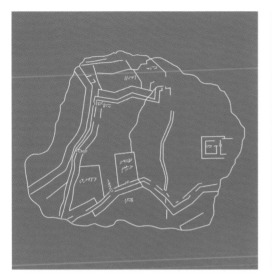

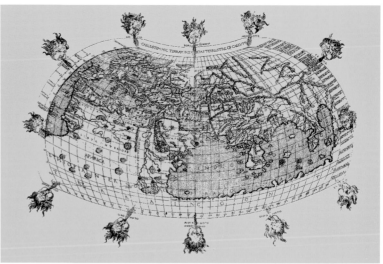

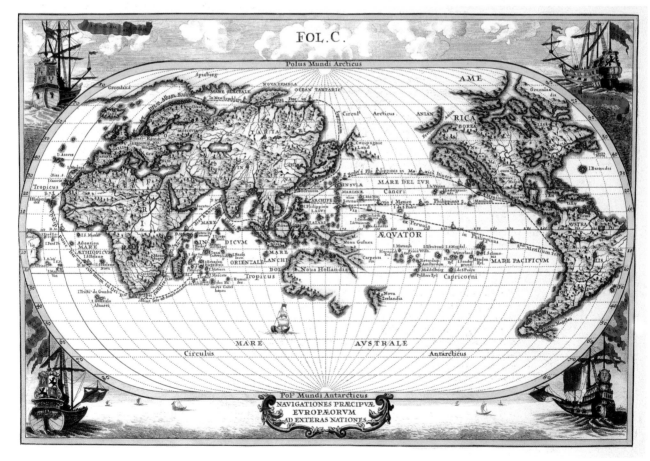

The marriage of cartography and technology has delivered entirely new mapping experiences, like this interactive satellite model of Earth (a collaboration between NASA and Google Earth™) that allows viewers to virtually fly to any location—perhaps even your street.

Satellite map services are now available on almost any web-enabled device.

Innovation: Charts and Graphs

While the precise dates for the first cave paintings, petroglyphs, and maps are difficult to trace, most historians credit a single person with the origins of charts and graphs.

William Playfair was a Scottish engineer and political economist who believed that the visualization of data was, in some cases, easier to understand than the written word. Playfair wrote two books, *The Commercial and Political Atlas* in 1786 and *The Statistical Breviary* in 1801, which used graphical representations of numeric data.[1] Playfair wanted his audience to be able to visualize the connections between economic factors. Instead of using tables of data as had been done previously, Playfair created line graphs, bar graphs, and pie charts which he then colored by hand. Playfair's designs enabled the reader to gain an improved understanding of quantities relative to one another and to see economic patterns over time.

Impact

The father of almost all modern charts and graphs, Playfair's visualization of data bridged significant knowledge gaps. Specialized skills were no longer needed to interpret complex numerical or statistical information, making it far more widely accessible, and data sets could be compared easily.

The next time you get paid to design the financial summary in an annual report, thank William Playfair.

1. A reproduction of both books, combined into a single volume, is published by Cambridge University Press.

↓
It's hard to imagine information design without charts and graphs. Their invention is primarily credited to one man, William Playfair. Perhaps more surprisingly, they were not created until the late eighteenth and early nineteenth centuries.

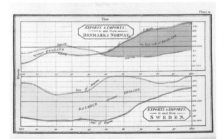

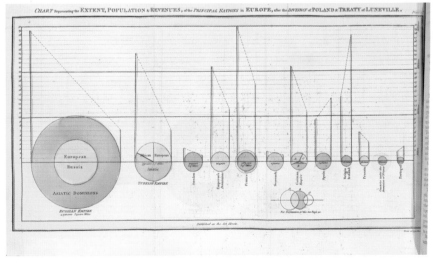

Innovation: ISOTYPE

ISOTYPE, short for International System of Typographic Picture Education, was an attempt to develop a standardized visual language.

ISOTYPE was created by Austrian sociologist and political economist Otto Neurath in 1940, with the help of German artist Gerd Arntz. Neurath's goal was to educate a broad audience by presenting complex socioeconomic data via easily understood symbols. Neurath believed that "words make division, pictures make connections," and that information should be accessible, regardless of education or cultural background. ISOTYPE was used primarily in the display of statistical information, in combination with traditional charts and graphs. Neurath's wife, Marie, also utilized ISOTYPE in books for children, creating visual sentences and narratives by stringing the images together.

Comprising over 1,000 different images, Neurath also developed a set of rules to ensure ISOTYPE's consistent application. These governed the use of color, orientation, the addition of text, and more. The ideas leading to the development and standardized use of ISOTYPE are referred to as the Vienna method of statistical display, which was widely used in Europe between 1940 and 1965. Its use eventually began to fade because of labor-intensive and expensive production, as each diagram had to be configured by hand using the printing technology of the time.

Impact

ISOTYPE's impact on contemporary information design is evident in the abundant application of internationally recognized icons. While Neurath's utopian vision for a universally adopted visual language never came to complete fruition, many of the symbols that we see in airports, museums, and public transit have their origins in this idea.

→
ISOTYPE, created by Otto Neurath in the 1940s, offered a standardized visual language. It was applied to a spectrum of topics with the intention of making complex data accessible to the masses, regardless of educational background.

ISOTYPE was also used in books for children. This example, from James Fisher's Adventure of the World, *depicts various climates and the appropriate attire for each.*

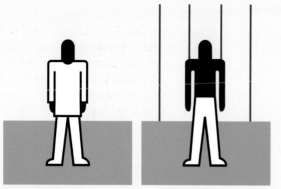

PRAIRIE
cool winter, warm summer

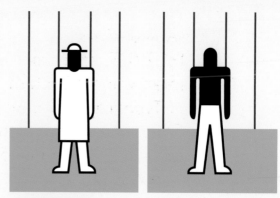

MARITIME
cool winter, warm summer

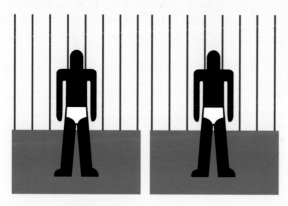

WET TROPICAL
very hot all the year

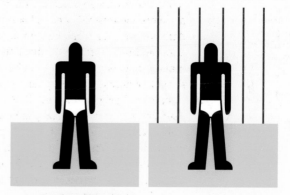

DRY TROPICAL
very hot all the year

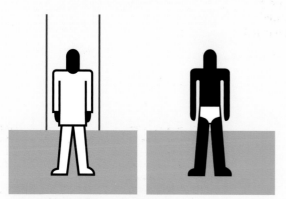

SEMI-DESERT (COOL)
cool winter, very hot summer

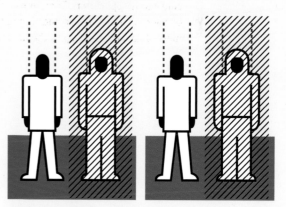

MOUNTAIN
very cold night, mild day

*Here, ISOTYPE is used to depict the differences between the American and British electoral systems (*Our Two Democracies, 1944*); map industrial and leisure locations across the globe (*Industrial and Holiday Centres*); and outline the weekly earnings of men and women by profession (*Women and Work, 1945*).*

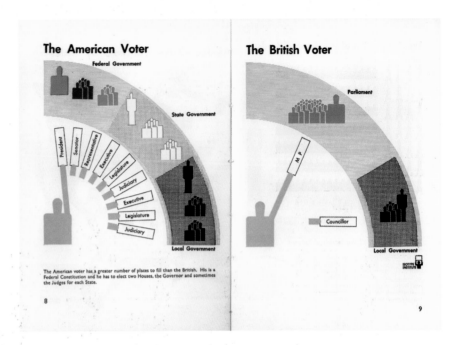

The American Voter

Federal Government

State Government

President
Senator
Representative
Executive
Legislature
Judiciary

Executive
Legislature
Judiciary

Local Government

The American voter has a greater number of places to fill than the British. His is a Federal Constitution and he has to elect two Houses, the Governor and sometimes the Judges for each State.

8

The British Voter

Parliament

M P

Councillor

Local Government

9

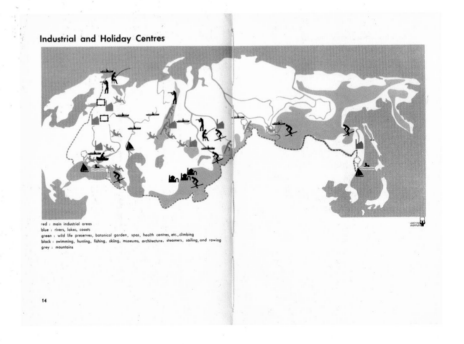

Industrial and Holiday Centres

red : main industrial areas
blue : rivers, lakes, coasts
green : wild life preserves, botanical garden, spas, health centres, etc., climbing
black : swimming, hunting, fishing, skiing, museums, architecture, steamers, sailing, and rowing
grey : mountains

14

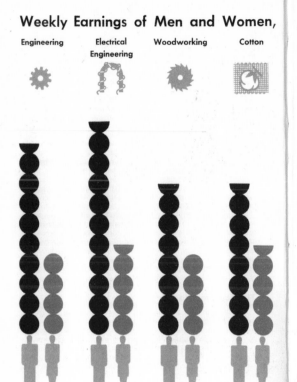

Weekly Earnings of Men and Women, 1940

CHART V

| Engineering | Electrical Engineering | Woodworking | Cotton | Hosiery | Dressmaking, Millinery | Food, drink, tobacco | Teachers elementary schools, provinces |

Each circle represents 10 shillings

blue: average weekly wages or middle salaries per week of men
red: average weekly wages or middle salaries per week of women

ISOTYPE INSTITUTE

Innovation: Guides for Structuring Information

Czech modernist Ladislav Sutnar is considered to be one of the great pioneers of information design.

Educated at the Prague School of the Decorative Arts, he became a professor at 26 and the director of the Prague State School of Graphic Arts a decade later. In addition, Sutnar was a practitioner, working in exhibition design, textiles, product design, and print. Sutnar's work was dominated by strict, functional typographic grids, sans-serif typefaces, white space, and the whimsical use of color and form.

Sutnar was responsible for the interior and exhibition design of the Czechoslovakian Pavilion at the New York World's Fair in 1939, which brought him to the United States. During the fair, Hitler's armies invaded Czechoslovakia and Sutnar made the decision to remain in the US. Upon emigrating, he was hired by the FW Dodge corporation as the Design Director of Research for Sweet's Catalog, a catalog service for architects and members of the building trades. At Sweet's, Sutnar met Knud Lönberg-Holm, an architect and author who became Sutnar's greatest collaborator. Together Sutnar and Lönberg-

Holm standardized every facet of Sweet's numerous catalogs and developed innovative systems for organizing, structuring, and displaying information, making the documents much easier to use. Sutnar would design in spreads rather than single pages (the dominant format of the period) and use parentheses, brackets, small images, and icons to reinforce hierarchical structures of content. These visual indexes allowed for rapid scanning of the page and enabled the reader to find information quickly.

Impact

Sutnar's methodical approach to structuring content, in conjunction with the use of spreads, may seem simple, but it proved revolutionary in its application and has been widely adopted in both print and digital media. His inventive use of parentheses, brackets, and other typographic details helps the reader visually compartmentalize data. In fact, Sutnar is credited with placing the parentheses around American area codes while working for the Bell Telephone Company. This seemingly minor detail is now a part of American visual vernacular.

Ladislav Sutnar's use of brackets, icons, and linear elements to organize content was a precursor to contemporary information design structures.

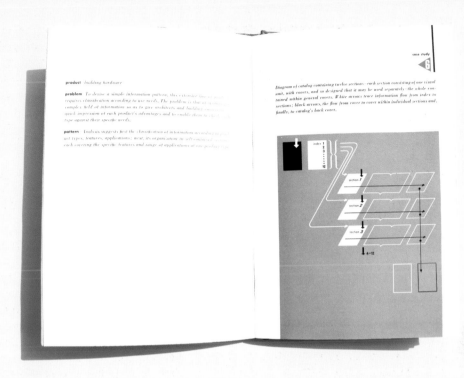

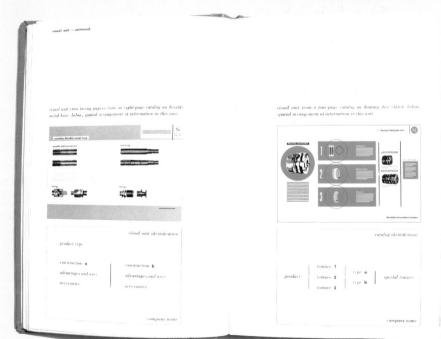

Innovation: The Interactive Exhibit

Most often remembered for their contributions to furniture design and film, Charles and Ray Eames were well ahead of their time in many creative efforts—including information and exhibition design.

The couple's first major commission in this area was *Mathematica: A World of Numbers and Beyond*, designed in 1961. Approached by the IBM corporation to design for the California Museum of Science and Industry, the Eameses created a 3,000ft² (278.7m²) exhibit that explained heady mathematical concepts using graphic displays and interactive experiences. Central to their theme was the notion that math could be fun. Nine interactive displays demonstrated the laws of probability, multiplication, celestial mechanics, and other complex topics. The Eameses engaged museumgoers by creating interactive spaces that required visitor participation. In the Probability Machine, for example, a button pressed by the patron would cause 30,000 plastic balls to fall into a screen and create a bell curve. Enclosing the exhibit were the History Wall, a timeline tracing the use of math through the ages, and the Image Wall, which contained visualizations of mathematical theory. The success of *Mathematica* led to many more notable commissions for Charles and Ray Eames, including the IBM Pavilion for the 1964 World's Fair and *The World of Franklin and Jefferson*, an exhibit and film created to celebrate the United States Bicentennial.

Impact

Today, the experiential concepts developed by Charles and Ray Eames have permeated contemporary museum and exhibit design, and even retail spaces. A visit to any local museum will testify to the transformative powers of interaction and play on contemporary exhibit design. You can still experience *Mathemetica* today; it remains on display at the Boston Museum of Science.

→

Mathematica: A World of Numbers and Beyond was the first prominent exhibition produced by the Eames Office. Its goal was to communicate complex mathematical theory in simple terms and engage and entertain museumgoers.

Shown here:

A boy peers through the Interactive Multiplication Cube.

The Eames Office also created short films for the exhibit, known as the Mathemetica Peepshows. Here two patrons sit and watch the shows.

Mathematica: A World of Numbers and Beyond *was the first prominent exhibition produced by the Eames Office. Its goal was to communicate complex mathematical theory in simple terms and engage and entertain museumgoers.*

Shown here:

Patrons explore the History Wall.

A family contemplates the bell curve created by the Probability Machine.

Innovation: The *Pioneer* Plaque

Most definitions of information design include language such as "design for human use" or "human-centered." But what happens when the intended audience isn't mankind?

Launched on March 2, 1972, by the National Aeronautics and Space Administration (NASA) of the United States, *Pioneer 10* was the first man-made artifact to travel beyond the boundaries of our solar system and into interstellar space. The last contact with *Pioneer 10* was made in January 2003, at which time the craft was 10 billion miles away from Earth.

While *Pioneer 10* is important for numerous scientific reasons, it also transports an example of information design intended as possible first contact with alien life. Attached to the exterior of the spacecraft is a 6 × 9in (15 × 23cm) gold anodized aluminum plate carrying a message about the spacecraft's creators. This communiqué, called The *Pioneer* Plaque, was designed by Frank Drake and Carl Sagan, both astronomers and astrophysicists (the artwork was produced by Sagan's wife, Linda Salzman Sagan). Descriptions of the spacecraft's creators, its launch date, and the location of Earth and its solar system are etched onto the plaque. Anatomical illustrations of a man and a woman are superimposed on a graphic of the spacecraft itself to indicate scale. The man's hand is raised in a symbol of greeting and welfare (NASA used similar plaques on Voyager missions with the female figure's hand raised

in greeting). Across the bottom of the panel are depictions of the planets in our solar system, also indicating launch and trajectory for the spacecraft.

Intersecting dashed lines on the panel attempt to pinpoint our solar system in relation to 14 pulsars (neutron stars that emit radio waves). To communicate this complex information without a common language, Frank and Sagan used the hydrogen atom (thought to be the most abundant element in the universe) as a map key for this pulsar illustration. They assumed that any life-form encountering *Pioneer 10* in space would be familiar with the atomic structure of hydrogen (one electron rotating around a single proton). They used an illustration of this element in a single rotation to create an icon for a singular unit, or the value of 1. That hydrogen key then provides a means of measurement for the radio waves emitted by the illustrated pulsars. Our solar system is located at the center of those pulsars. So, what may appear to be a starburst is actually an interstellar map.

Impact

The *Pioneer* Plaque's success as a means of interstellar communication remains to be seen. However, the perceived value of its mission is still embraced by NASA—similar plaques have been placed on all subsequent interstellar space probes. At the turn of the millennium, NASA engaged 300 artists to submit work for the development of a new plaque, exploring holographic technology as a more information-dense medium.

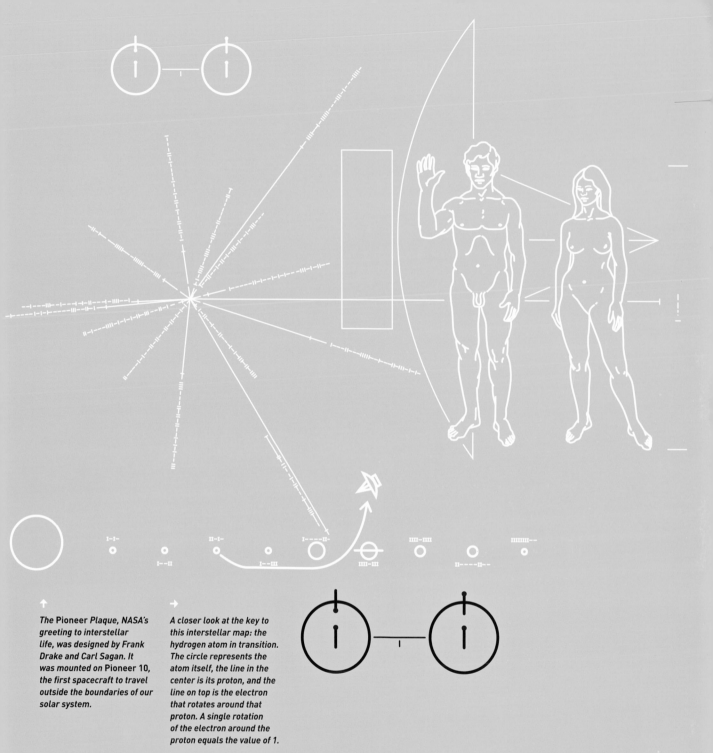

The Pioneer Plaque, NASA's greeting to interstellar life, was designed by Frank Drake and Carl Sagan. It was mounted on Pioneer 10, the first spacecraft to travel outside the boundaries of our solar system.

A closer look at the key to this interstellar map: the hydrogen atom in transition. The circle represents the atom itself, the line in the center is its proton, and the line on top is the electron that rotates around that proton. A single rotation of the electron around the proton equals the value of 1.

Innovation: The Visible Language Workshop

Acclaimed as one of the most influential designers of the 20th century, Muriel Cooper and her work with the Visible Language Workshop at the Massachusetts Institute of Technology's Media Lab have helped frame our contemporary digital experience.

After accepting a position as an Art Director at MIT Press in 1967, Cooper attended a computer programming workshop led by Nicholas Negroponte (with whom she would later cofound the MIT Media Lab). She felt bewildered by the nonvisual approach to human–computer interaction and the cumbersome manual coding of computer languages. Cooper was a very highly regarded book designer, winning over 100 awards and designing over 500 titles, but this workshop led her to see the vast, unexplored potential that new technology held for graphic design. In 1974, Cooper began teaching a class called Messages and Means with Ronald MacNeil (another future collaborator). Together they investigated the relationship between graphic design and technology, laying the foundation for the Visible Language Workshop, where designers, programmers, and computer scientists would come together in a spirit of exploration and experimentation. Cooper became an official member of the MIT faculty in 1978 and eventually one of the founding members of its Media Lab (arguably the premier think tank of the digital revolution), where she would house her now-esteemed Visual Language Workshop.

It is often said that Cooper's legacy in the field of design is not the artifacts that she created, but the inspiration she gave to Media Lab students. Focusing on developing new ways to interact with and organize content and typography within a digital space, Cooper was a pioneer in interactive design—even though she knew little about programming.

Impact

A huge influence on a generation of some of the brightest students on Earth, the Visual Language Workshop's impact is felt in many of today's interactive digital environments. Its visionary, Muriel Cooper, exposed the potential of a marriage between design and technology, encouraged enthusiastic cooperation between diverse specialists, and ultimately created interactive experiences that were more functional—and better still, more meaningful. Cooper's Media Lab colleague Nicholas Negroponte said: "The impact of Muriel's work can be summed up in two words: Beyond Windows. It will be seen as the turning point in interface design. She has broken the flatland of overlapping opaque rectangles with the idea of a galactic universe."[1]

1. Nicholas Negroponte's quote is from the AIGA Medalist biography of Muriel Cooper at http://aiga.org/content.cfm/medalist-murielcooper

Examples of student work from the Visual Language Workshop at MIT. Founded by designer Muriel Cooper, the Workshop encouraged collaboration between science and art, and supported wild, often innovative experimentation. These projects, and those featured on the next two pages, illustrate a visionary approach to computer interactivity.

Muriel Cooper at the MIT Visible Language Workshop.

17.18

.40

78

0.87

0.97

0.91

21.53

25.99

6.07

17.47

18.01

-0.21

22.61

5

MStar Rating: 2.90

Avg. MStar Rtg.: **2.90**

178 Total Mos. Rtd.: **178**

MStar Risk 3yr: **0.64**
1.12

MStar Risk 5yr: **0.85**
1.23

MStar Risk 10yr: **0.93**
1.29

Ytd. Total Rtn.: **9.01**

43.58

Yr. Total Rtn.: **18.95**
4.00

178

0.64

0.89

0.81

14.09

27.73

26.18

48.22

1.60

1.65

NA

13.70

-5.11

1.11

17.94

17.47

1992 Annual Rtn: **26.99**
24.23
99.08 18.03

1991 Annual Rtn: **31.51**
47.35
84.91

1990 Annual Rtn: **-7.84**

1989 Annual Rtn: **41.64**
17.71
21.66
24.70

1988 Annual Rtn: **15.69**
-0.30 4.44

1987 Annual Rtn: **-8.02**
3.17
16.82
55.41
15.89

1986 Annual Rtn: **9.61**
31.55

1985 Annual Rtn: **43.40**

1984 Annual Rtn: **15.48**
25.29
46.15

1983 A **25.10**

11.06

Inc. Ratio: **0.8**
0.59
0.90

Price/Earn Ratio: **14.2**
32.65
26.79

Rtn. on Assets: **6.9**

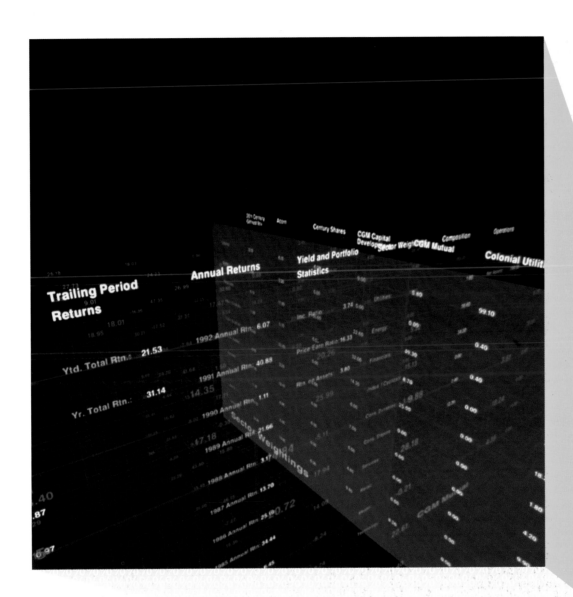

Innovation: The First Website

Computers have had the ability to communicate via telephone lines and modems for over 50 years.

However, the concept of the internet as we know it today was developed in 1989 by Tim Berners-Lee, a physicist working at CERN, the European Organization for Nuclear Research (originally Conseil Européen pour la Recherche Nucléaire). Berners-Lee proposed connecting hypertext (links embedded in on-screen text that connect the user to other documents or files) to the internet so that researchers could share information more quickly. He was joined by Robert Cailliau, a systems engineer at CERN, and the pair built the first web browser, editor, server, and web page on a NeXT computer. They also coined the phrase "World Wide Web." The first address on the web was http://info.cern.ch/hypertext/WWW/TheProject.html, a page explaining the technology behind the web, how to build a website, and how to undertake an effective search. Realizing that the NeXT machines being used at CERN were more powerful than the average personal computer, they developed a browser that was universally compatible and distributed that technology for free. Web servers and sites emerged across Europe and

the United States. In February 1993, Marc Andreessen, a student at the National Center for Supercomputing Applications (NCSA) at the University of Illinois, released Mosaic, a browser that could also display image files. Mosaic would eventually lead Andreessen to develop Netscape Communications Corporation, where the internet revolution would begin in earnest.

Impact

In the short time since the release of Mosaic, websites have changed the way we do everything: conduct business, consume media, shop, interact with friends and family, maybe even find a spouse! With rates of digital inclusion on the rise throughout the world, it is evident that we are making new connections at an exponential rate. Those in the technology sector often pat themselves on the back for opening the floodgates of the world's knowledge, but it is not a story of technology alone. In its earliest forms, the web was an austere tool used primarily by the scientific community. Fuel for the revolution was the practical application of a user-centered graphic interface. Designers were able to harness the potential of this new tool and forge it into something that people could use. Websites started to look, feel, and function in familiar contexts—all of a sudden you could see a picture of a sweater, zoom in for a closer look, and place it into a shopping cart to make your purchase. Technology is only half of the equation. Lacking the value created by the information design community, public acceptance of the web might have been an uphill struggle.

The first website was hosted by CERN, a nuclear research organization. It was viewed on a line-mode browser, which could only display text. Imagine your current use of the internet in this format.

The user-friendly interface of the Netscape Navigator 1.0 browser was instrumental in the development of the web.

CERN Welcome

CERN

The European Laboratory for Particle Physics, located near Geneva[1] in
Switzerland[2] and France [3]. Also the birthplace of the World-Wide
Web[4].

This is the CERN laboratory main server. The support team provides a set of
Services[5] to the physics experiments and the lab. For questions and
suggestions, see WWW Support Contacts[6] at CERN

About the Laboratory[7] — Hot News[8] — Activities[9] — About Physics[10] —
  Other Subjects[11] — Search [12]

About the Laboratory

        Help[13] and General information[14], divisions, groups and
        activities[15] (structure), Scientific committees [16]

        Directories[17] (phone & email, services & people), Scientific
        Information Service[18] (library, archives or Alice) Preprint[19] Server

1—45, Back, Up, <RETURN> for more, Quit, or Help:

Principles

Designers take inspiration from numerous sources: popular culture, nature, art. While studying science might not seem as romantic, it yields results. To understand the end user so that we can target our messaging, we need to learn more about how they will receive and decode the information sets we send. Though designers need not become behavioral scientists, knowledge of the principles framing cognition, communication, and aesthetics provides

This section explores the connections and convergences between human perception, thinking, and learning; how we transmit knowledge, share concepts, and process information through language; and how structure and legibility affect the visualization of messaging. These theories, identified and tested by academics and professionals, support the design decisions you make on a daily basis.

The goal of any information design task is to communicate a specific message to the end user in a way that is clear, accessible, and easy to understand.

In order to accomplish this task the designer spends hours researching subject matter and intended audience; exploring creative, conceptual, technical, and production issues; and finally, carefully crafting that message with rhetoric, imagery, typography, layout, and form.

The study of human perception, thinking, and learning can provide the designer with crucial insight into the needs of the end user. Even an elementary understanding of cognitive science and educational theory can make a big difference in the way aesthetic decisions are made. In this chapter we'll focus on the way individuals interpret and acquire new knowledge by investigating learning styles and cognitive processes with immediate implications for visual communication.

Learning Styles

There are many different theories within the educational and cognitive science communities regarding the processes and motivations that drive the way people learn. These models vary in complexity, yet it is largely agreed that all individuals prefer some particular sensory method (or mode) of experiencing, interacting with, and remembering new information. These predispositions are called "learning styles." In educational studies, Rita and Kenneth Dunn's exploration of learning styles in the 1970s was highly influential.[1] Since that time numerous educators and psychologists have contributed to the discussion. The three most common learning styles are Visual, Auditory/Verbal, and Kinesthetic/Tactile.

Visual

Visual learners prefer images when encountering new information. They are more likely to remember information when it has been presented in the form of a picture, map, chart, or film. Visual learners create flowcharts, diagrams, or other forms of graphic organization to master new knowledge. People who learn best by seeing new information often think in terms of movies or pictures rather than words. As such, visual learners tend to have a strong awareness of aesthetics and space.

Auditory/Verbal

Verbal learners prefer experiencing new information in the form of written and spoken words. Individuals exhibiting this learning style prefer information presented in the form of lectures, written documents, and group discussion. They study by reading, writing notes, listening, and talking. Auditory/Verbal learners tend to think in words rather than pictures and often have strong written and verbal communication skills.

1. The Dunn and Dunn Learning-Style Model has been widely studied and applied to all levels of academia and education since the 1970s.

2. See the Eameses'
Mathematica exhibit in
Chapter 3 for an excellent
example of this theory in
practice (p. 40).

↗
Visual learners:
· *Learn best from images*
· *Think in terms of pictures*
· *Possess a strong aesthetic
  sense*

Auditory/Verbal learners:
· *Learn best from using
  language*
· *Think in terms of words*
· *Possess strong written and
  verbal skills*

Kinesthetic/Tactile learners:
· *Learn best by doing*
· *Work well with their hands*
· *Possess good physical
  coordination*

Kinesthetic/Tactile

Kinesthetic learners acquire knowledge by doing. These individuals need to physically experience new information by using large and small muscle groups, and need to touch and feel content. They prefer labs, demonstrations, and learning through play. Kinesthetic/Tactile learners will act out skits, role-play, or devise other forms of physical manipulation to master new skills. Individuals exhibiting this learning style tend to work well with their hands and are physically coordinated.

Different learning styles suit our developmental needs at different times of our lives. Most of us learn best through a combination of educational experiences, but each individual tends toward a particular learning style as he or she reaches adulthood. While noting the unique needs of the individual, it is also sometimes possible to predict the general learning styles of an audience by assessing clues such as professions, skills, and hobbies. Armed with a simple understanding of the human learning process, the information designer is better able to communicate with the target audience. It is important to remember that most people learn through a combination of styles. By incorporating supporting layers of information in the form of type, images, and, when possible, tactile and aural experiences, the designer is able to engage multiple stimuli, creating a more memorable and meaningful experience.[2]

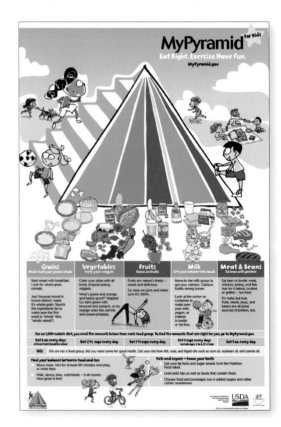

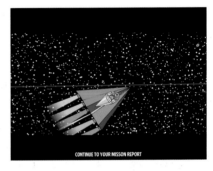

←↑

Designers can address different learning styles by targeting messages for each specific audience. In this example of instructional materials used by the US Department of Agriculture to teach healthy eating habits to children, the multiple learning styles are addressed through different artifacts. A poster contains illustrations and text-heavy charts, which should appeal to visual and verbal learners. A video game creates a more interactive and kinesthetic experience, allowing the user to "virtually" plan a day of meals and exercise in order to fuel a rocket.

Process

Memory

Memory is a cognitive process that enables us to store, retrieve, and apply knowledge. Educators and psychologists have spent years studying human information processing and how it relates to our ability to remember that information. Designers can take an important cue from these efforts.

The Stage Theory Model

One widely accepted framework for understanding this fundamental process is The Stage Theory Model.[1]

This model asserts that human memory develops in three specific stages: sensory input, short-term memory, and long-term memory.

A simplified explanation of the Stage Theory Model outlines the creation of memory in terms of notice, storage, and retrieval. The process works like this:

Sensory Input (Notice): Our senses recognize and momentarily store incoming environmental stimuli in sensory memory. At this point, the brain either filters out (ignores and forgets) the new stimuli or passes that information into the short-term memory. With visual stimuli, the human mind holds imagery in a type of sensory memory known as iconic memory. In milliseconds that information is transferred to a short-term memory store.

Short-term Memory (Storage): When information has entered the short-term memory we are able to begin processing it in an active and conscious way. Once again, we have the option to discard the new information or continue thinking about it.

[1] Sensory Input

The more we process that information, the more likely it is that we will remember it later. We are capable of storing information in the short-term memory for about 20–30 seconds before it is either forgotten or entered into the long-term memory.

Long-term Memory (Storage and Retrieval):
The long-term memory works like a permanent depository where information is stored and retrieved when it is needed. Information stored in the long-term memory is stored indefinitely.

The Stage Theory Model postulates that memories develop in three specific stages. First, an individual notices sensory input (an image, a sound, etc.). That input is quickly moved to the short-term memory. With sufficient rehearsal or mental processing (called a feedback loop) it enters the long-term memory, where it will be stored indefinitely for later retrieval.

1. The Stage Theory Model is also known as the Atkinson and Shiffrin Model.

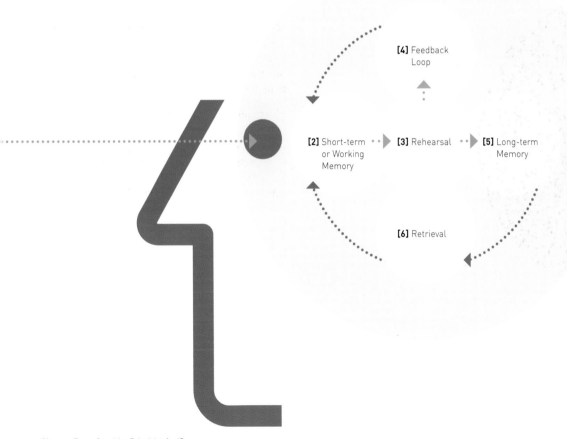

[4] Feedback Loop

[2] Short-term or Working Memory

[3] Rehearsal

[5] Long-term Memory

[6] Retrieval

Process

Memory

Miller's Magic Number

Related to the study of short-term memory, cognition, and perception is the theory of Miller's Magic Number,[1] or chunking.

George Miller, a psychology professor at Harvard University in the 1950s, wanted to identify the limits of short-term memory. Through a series of experiments Miller discovered that the capacity for short-term memory varied among individuals, but that it was possible to measure it in "chunks." A chunk is any single unit of information. Miller's research revealed that the human brain could remember seven chunks, plus or minus two, in the short-term memory. It is possible to remember larger amounts of content by rechunking or recoding—the act of grouping sets of information into a single unit and then combining those units using the "Magical Number 7, +/-2." Of course, the more familiar the subject is with the core content, the easier it is to remember greater quantities. Chunking is also associated with memory aids such as mnemonics. Consider "Roy G. Biv," a common mnemonic device or abbreviation for remembering the colors of the rainbow, or visible light spectrum. Each letter in the fictional Roy G. Biv's name represents a color in the correct sequence: red, orange, yellow, green, blue, indigo, and violet. Technically that list of seven colors falls within Miller's range of easily memorized quantities, but by rechunking the units into three parts (a first name, middle initial, and last name) we're more likely to retain the proper order and quickly pair it with our previous knowledge of color names.

1. To read the original paper on chunking, see "The Magical Number Seven, Plus or Minus Two: Some Limits on our Capacity for Processing Information," by George A. Miller, *The Psychological Review*, 1956, vol. 63, pp. 81–97.

4408675309
(440) 867–5309

ROY G BIV

↑
The application of Miller's Magic Number can be easily visualized by considering something as commonplace as a telephone number. Take a quick glance at the list of 10 consecutive numbers. Easy to remember? Now look at the same numbers broken into the three-part configuration familiar to US citizens (with the area code bracketed, thanks to Ladislav Sutnar). Easier to recall? That's because the information has been rechunked into just three sets.

↑
Miller's Magic Number is often related to the use of mnemonic devices. Here, the colors of the visible light spectrum are reduced to a simple name, Roy G. Biv. Each letter represents a specific color, listed in the correct order.

For communication theories that relate to memory,
read the following sections of Chapter 5:
- *AIDA (Attention, Interest, Desire, Action) (p. 80)*
- *The Principle of Least Effort (p. 86)*
- *Literacy (p. 91)*

For information on how grids can help to visually
chunk information sets, read Chapter 6:
- *Structure (p. 98)*

Quick Tips

Design for retention

Make aesthetic and communication
decisions that target every stage of the
memory process. Use contrasts and
color to attract immediate notice. Create
associations with familiar subjects to help
the user store the information. And provide
parsed, accessible chunks of content for
easy retrieval.

Make it easy

Use Miller's Magic Number to make
complex information sets easier for your
user to access, understand, and recall.
Break complicated or lengthy content into
smaller chunks, always remembering "7,
+/-2" as your guide. Then utilize design
continuity to link those sections into a
broader message.

Process

Perception and
Discernment

Perception—our ability to rapidly absorb and assess stimuli from our environment—is interlinked with discernment. The latter allows us to comprehend a stimulus and then distinguish it from others. Studying the "why" of perception and discernment from a cognitive perspective can help designers target their messages for maximum reception.

1. Numerous studies have confirmed the validity of Weber's Law. It should be noted, however, that difference thresholds, as defined by Weber, don't apply when stimulus reaches extreme levels.

Difference Threshold

Sensory stimuli—anything from the brightness of a light to the volume of a sound to the saltiness of food—are subject to modulation.

How quickly we, as receivers, take note of these changes is of interest to cognitive psychologists, social scientists, and marketeers alike. Weber's Law of Just Noticeable Differences defines the minimum amount of change required in any type of sensory stimulus for an individual to take notice.

Weber's Law postulates that the amount of change, once determined, remains a constant and can be predicted for future stimuli. For example, if a viewer is shown a type specimen that is 10 points in size, and the next noticeable change in size that they recognize is at 12 points, the rate of change is equal to 2 points. This change is known as the

1-point Difference	2-point Difference
Garamond 9pt	Garamond 9pt
Garamond 10pt	Garamond 11pt
Garamond 11pt	Garamond 13pt
Garamond 12pt	Garamond 15pt
Garamond 13pt	
Garamond 14pt	
Garamond 15pt	

"difference threshold," and as the value of the stimulus increases, the difference threshold remains the same. Therefore, according to Weber's Law, subsequent change would be apparent at 14 points, 16 points, 18 points, and so on.[1]

Weber's Law has been applied to many different types of sensory experiences, and rates of just noticeable difference are predominantly consistent for all subjects tested within a specific query. When determining difference thresholds, as with any other quantitative study, the more users are tested, the more accurate the results.

The spirit of Weber's Law can be applied during the creation of visual communication projects, helping designers make constructive choices. Put to use when developing a type system, the difference threshold can help to determine contrasts in size, weight, and leading, ensuring that the information follows an obvious hierarchy. By spending a little time on user testing early in the process, a designer's intuition regarding aesthetic decisions can be confirmed. Checking visual assumptions with Weber's Law establishes clear communication with the audience.

Weber's Law can be applied to typographic study to determine noticeable changes in both weight and size. While designers are often attuned to subtle changes in type, to a broader audience those differences are often lost.

This list, showing various weights of the type family Meta, exemplifies the range of options available to designers. The selected Meta fonts on the right suggest increments of difference that an average audience might easily identify. This doesn't imply that those are the only font weights worth using, but rather that easily noticeable differentiation requires skipping a weight. The same rule applies to type size.

Process

Perception and
Discernment

The Gestalt Principles of Perception

Gestalt psychology views the workings of the human mind as a holistic process that strives to self-organize.

In the 1930s, Gestalt psychologists Kurt Koffka, Wolfgang Köhler, and Max Wertheimer applied this theory to visual perception. They believed that humans perceive compositions as a whole, rather than as a collection of individual forms. While individual design elements might possess unique information, when they are viewed in relation to other elements their meaning and context changes. Koffka, Köhler, and Wertheimer theorized that in terms of visual perception, understanding is achieved by recognizing the interplay between design elements and concurrently reading the composition as a whole. Their experiments in visual perception sought to describe how we group multiple elements into complete compositions.

The results of these studies formed what are now commonly referred to as the Gestalt Principles of Perception. These principles give support to many of the techniques designers use to manipulate forms and create hierarchy and meaning.

The most relevant are listed below:

The Principle of Proximity states that when viewers see adjacent objects they process them as a group, and consider them to have like meaning.

The Principle of Similarity states that objects which share similar attributes—such as size, color, shape, direction, orientation, weight, and texture—are perceptually and cognitively grouped together.

The Principle of Prägnanz, also known as the figure–ground relationship, states that when looking at a visual field, objects appear either dominant or recessive. Dominant objects are perceived as figures, and recessive objects are seen as background. When images or patterns are reversible it becomes hard to differentiate the figure–ground relationship. A related concept is the Principle of Area, which dictates that smaller objects are generally perceived as figures in a larger visual field or background.

The Principle of Closure states that we mentally close up or form objects that are visually implied. For example, a series of adjacent points forms a visually implied line—the viewer sees the line rather than the individual dots.

→ →
This highway sign (near right), indicating directions to two interstate exchanges, may be difficult for many viewers to read quickly. Using the Principles of Proximity and Similarity, we can determine what is leading to the confusion. Both signs are of *similar shape, size, color, and typographic content, and are placed in very close proximity. A possible redesign (far right) to address legibility at high speeds while still maintaining a cohesive signage system would position the signs farther apart, enlarge the* *crucial differentiations between East and West, and enhance the contrast between the road numbers and the background.*

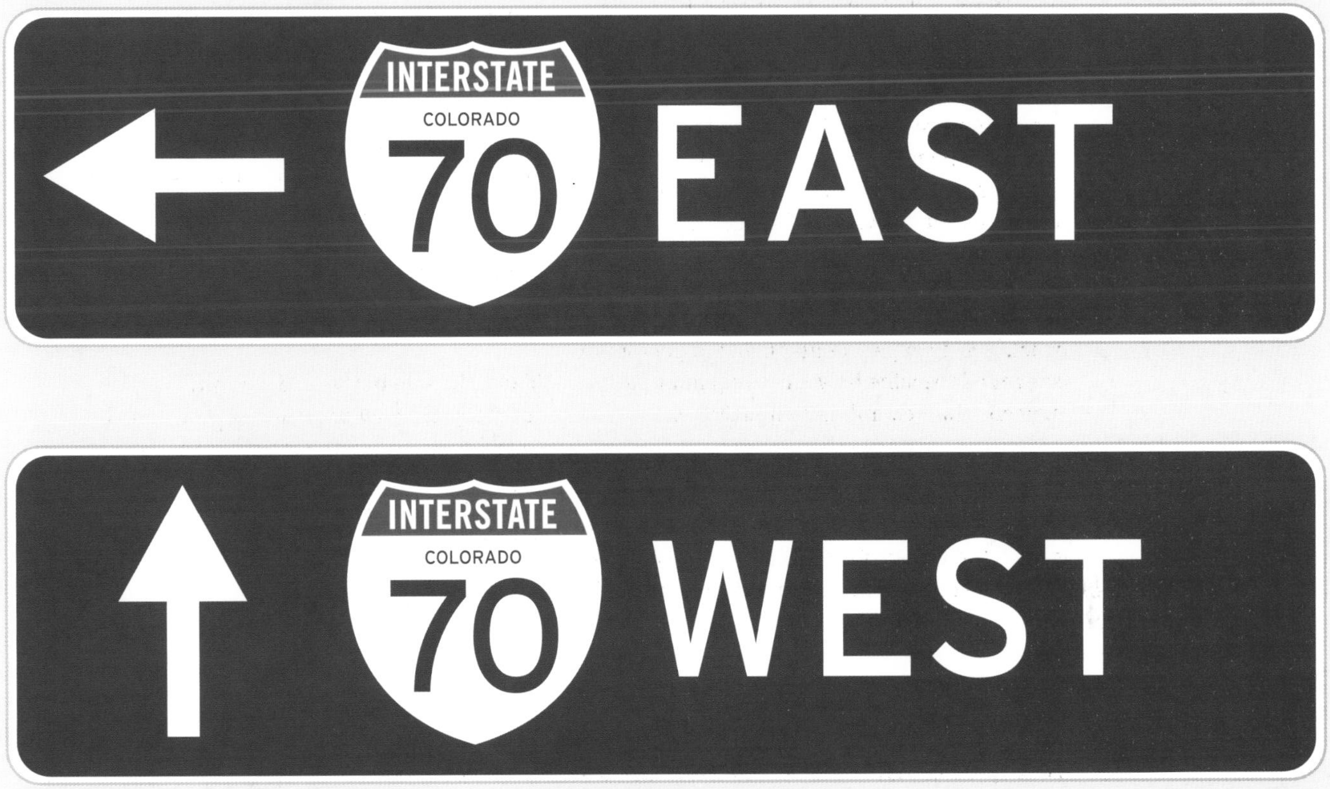
INTERSTATE
COLORADO
70
EAST
INTERSTATE
COLORADO
70
WEST

Eye Tracking

Scientists have discovered that human eyes are in perpetual motion, creating image data and transferring it to our brains.

Physiologically, if we were to able hold our eyes perfectly still the images would eventually fade away for want of fresh stimulus, so our eyes are in a constant state of motion to acquire and reacquire visual data.

Eye tracking, the study of where our gaze falls, measures several different eye movements. Behavioral scientists and usability engineers divide these movements into fixations, saccades, and scanpaths.

Fixation occurs when our eyes appear to pause in a certain position.

Saccade is the movement between one fixation and the next, or the movement that occurs when the eye changes position.

Scanpath is the term used to describe a series of fixations and saccades.

Researchers can track the location and duration of fixations, the number of subsequent saccades, and scanpath lengths to determine what test subjects are looking at, and for how long. These tests can be recorded and data from different subjects can be compared to determine whether there is any continuity in the users' experiences. Dominant fixation points are sometimes called "hot spots" and are considered to be prominent areas of interest. Research also indicates that the human eye has a tendency to follow the same scanpaths when encountering familiar imagery. In this situation unexpected or incongruous details become areas of fixation and distraction.

Applied research in eye tracking has been in use since the 1950s, but has seen a recent resurgence in popularity thanks to usability testing for websites and traditional advertising. The process can evaluate page layout or interface design. Scanpaths can be followed in real time to determine how long it takes users to perform specific tasks. This practice allows the research and design team to see through the eyes of the participant, gauging how much time they spend reading content and how quickly they move to different areas of a page—ultimately determining the success or failure of information delivery.

Fixation

Saccade

Scanpath

Applied research in eye tracking has been in use since the 1950s, but has seen a recent resurgence in popularity thanks to usability testing for websites and traditional advertising.

Test Subject 1

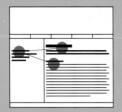

Test Subject 2

Test Subject 3

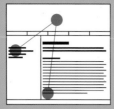

Test Subject 4

Test Subject 5

Test Subject 6

Test Subject 7

Test Subject 8

Test Subject 9

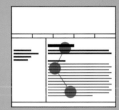

Test Subject 10

Our eyes don't read in a continuous steady line but rather scan information in a rapid series of movements. In this example, fixations, where the eye seems to pause, are represented by dots, and saccades, the movements that connect fixations, are represented by lines. The entire series of fixations and saccades is called a scanpath.

Marketing research firms and usability labs record the unique fixations, saccades, and scanpaths of several test subjects in order to determine where different areas of interest fall on a page. Each individual test is then superimposed to create a "heat map." Results from these studies can give the designer insight into the users' focus, confirming or questioning a planned visual hierarchy.

Superimposed View

Process

Perception and
Discernment

1. William S. Cleveland's research is primarily targeted at individuals designing for complex scientific and statistical data, rather than at a marketing communication audience. However, many of Cleveland's findings can apply to both. To learn more, in Cleveland's own words, read his book *Visualizing Data* (Hobart Press, 1993).

Perception of Graphic Statistical Displays: Cleveland's Task Model

The legibility of charts and graphs is of utmost concern to information designers.

But have you ever considered what kind of mental calculations occur when your readers process those statistical displays? William S. Cleveland, a professor of statistics and computer science at Purdue University, Indiana, has defined how we visually decode the content in graphic displays of statistical information[1]. The process he outlines has a direct impact on the artifacts information designers create.

Graphs tell two different stories. First, they make general statements, broad overviews like "The market was up this year," or "Annual rainfall was at a 20-year low." Second, they tell the tale of specific details, events, dates, numbers, or quantities, like "Trading volume peaked on December 12," or "The hurricane season of 2005 dropped more precipitation than that of 2006." The reader's mind processes the graph's content (or stories) in two different ways. Cleveland refers to these processes as Pattern Perception and Table Lookup.

When the user can see trends in the data or make broad, comprehensive conclusions about a graph's content, they are using pattern perception. In this process, the individual variables of the graph are not as important as an overall understanding of the content (the message all those variables create when grouped together). During pattern perception viewers may be able to define a single trend or see migrations of data in different directions. Pattern perception occurs rapidly, and provides the reader with an immediate overview of the graph's content.

Table lookup is a process that requires the reader to undertake a more detailed analysis of specific content. In this phase, the viewer is making determinations about a single subject (date, event, measurement, etc.) and its relationship to the rest of the measurements, graphic devices, and information on the graph. During table lookup the viewer may scan the legend or scales on the X and Y axes, assign value to a representative graphic, or compare and match symbols. The information being processed is a detail of the larger whole.

Design decisions ultimately determine the success or failure of pattern perception, table lookup, and the visualization's accuracy in relation to the original data set. Inaccurate designs can skew facts and alter concepts. Good typographic and aesthetic decisions can enhance scanning, help the user see relationships to scale, and ensure that symbols and other graphic devices are easily detected and identified. When creating visual displays of statistics, the information designer has two goals: be specific, clear and accurate; and give the audience a quick read.

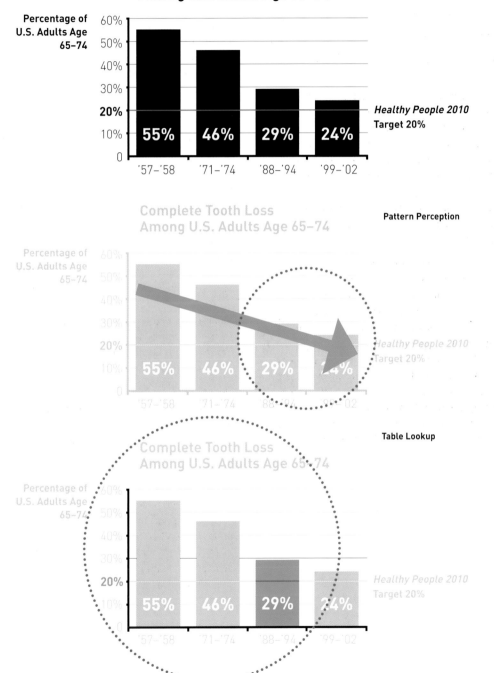

**Complete Tooth Loss
Among U.S. Adults Age 65–74**

Percentage of
U.S. Adults Age
65–74

60%
50%
40%
30%
20%
10%
0

55%   46%   29%   24%

'57–'58   '71–'74   '88–'94   '99–'02

Healthy People 2010
Target 20%

Pattern Perception

Table Lookup

*William S. Cleveland suggests
that users access two
different mental processes,
pattern perception and
table lookup, to decode the
data in charts and graphs.
During pattern perception,
we recognize overall trends.
In the example shown here,
pattern perception indicates
that the rate of complete
tooth loss for elderly US
citizens is going down.
When using table lookup,
individuals are focused on
specific data, and are using
detail-oriented information-
seeking strategies to gather
information. In our example,
they might be studying the
specifics for tooth loss from
1988–94.*

This *Architect* magazine article employs numerous charts and graphs to help the reader visualize trends in building. Note the use of linear elements and representative graphics to help the viewer quickly process information.

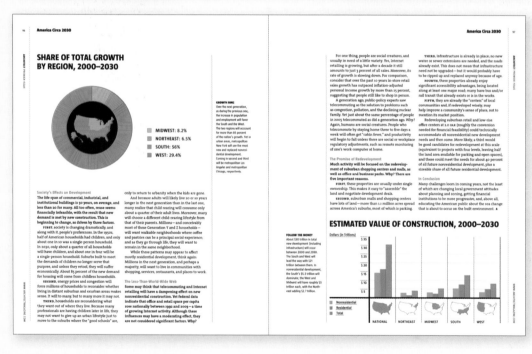

Quick Tips

More than "just noticeable" differences

Determining the difference threshold tells the designer where the audience will notice the smallest change. Take Weber's principle and magnify those just noticeable differences into really noticeable differences to ensure clear informational hierarchy.

Proven practices

Use the Gestalt Principles of Perception to influence hierarchy and reading order. Group objects to create contextual relationships. Use contrasts to separate ideas. Guide the viewer's eye through the content with implied alignments.

Keep things consistent

Use grids, flow-lines, and typography to create familiarity in layouts. Studies show that consistent placement of content creates scanpaths to which the viewer will soon become accustomed. This will then help them to process information more quickly.

Confirm with an expert

Use eye tracking to confirm aesthetic choices affecting hierarchy and focal points. Usability labs and marketing research firms provide a range of services and pricing if you don't have the technology or expertise in-house.

Design tasks

When designing charts and graphs, use dynamic color, value, and shape contrast to aid pattern perception. Assist the viewer with table lookup by clearly labeling X and Y axes, creating marked contrast for type and symbols representing different information sets, and delineating grids so that scale is clear.

For more information on how perception affects communication, read the following sections of Chapter 5:
- *LATCH (Location, Alphabet, Time, Category, Hierarchy) Organization (p. 82)*
- *The Principle of Least Effort (p. 86)*

For more information about how aesthetic choices affect perception, read Chapter 6.

Process

Wayfinding

The term "wayfinding"[1] describes how an individual orients him- or herself within a new environment, and the cognitive processes used to determine and follow a route, traversing from one point to the next.

It may refer to a physical journey (walking your pet to the new dog park), or a virtual one (navigating an online database), and may be familiar (driving to your childhood home) or unfamiliar (the transit system in a foreign city). As the individual contemplates directionality, a route emerges. Depending on the user and the complexity of navigation, this route is either committed to memory or recorded in writing, as a drawing, or digitally. The development of this route, at least initially a mental plan, will be influenced by environmental cues (landmarks, topography, established pathways), culture (gender roles, navigational anxieties, aesthetic preferences), and design (signs, directional elements, architecture, technology).

We orient spatially by employing two different knowledge sets. When individuals use environmental cues and landmarks to wayfind, they are utilizing "route-based knowledge." When they look at representations of space, such as maps, to choose their path, they are accessing "survey knowledge." Survey knowledge is especially important when encountering new environments. Route-based knowledge is more applicable to familiar paths, but not necessarily limited to those

situations. Some combination of the two provides the most successful method.

"Legibility" is the term used to define the ease with which wayfinding routes can be followed (a clear route has high legibility; a complicated route, low legibility).

Design can provide this clarity. As we consider the space we wish to traverse, it is helpful to visualize it in terms of points, lines, and planes. Points can be places (home, or a desired destination) or they can be signs or physical landmarks. Lines are the paths that lead us from one place to another, or perceived boundaries. Planes define large quantities of like information: neighborhoods, communities, cities, districts, regions, etc. This visual geometry helps us navigate physical, virtual, and conceptual environments. It explains why site maps can be as beneficial to internet users as a road atlas is to drivers.

Legibility can also be enhanced by increasing the clarity and visibility of signage, icons, and directional indicators at decision-making points along a route.

1. Most academics credit MIT professor Kevin Lynch with coining the term "wayfinding" in his book *The Image of the City* (MIT Press, 1960). Lynch was an urban planner who used wayfinding to describe how people navigated cities. In his studies he asked people to draw maps of their city from memory, and then compared these drawings to find the common features that appeared on the majority of the maps. Lynch's research lists paths, landmarks, regions, edges, and nodes as those common features.

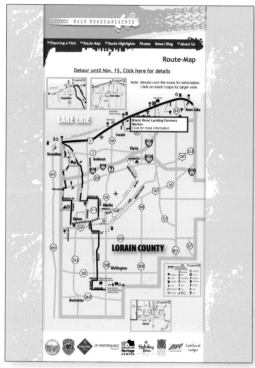

→
We use two different wayfinding strategies, usually in combination, to travel from one place to another. Route-based knowledge is information that is located or used along the way, like signs or landmarks. Survey knowledge requires users to look at a representation of a space—a map, for example. Back Roads and Beaches, a bicycle route that connects local communities, tourist destinations, and area beaches in Lorain County, Ohio, provides both print and digital maps so that riders can plan their trip, and clearly designated signs along roads and pathways to ensure they stay on the correct track.

Quick Tips

Provide a map
Some cognitive scientists argue that survey knowledge is the easiest and most efficient method of wayfinding. Include a map wherever possible to help users orient themselves within their environment.

Use well-defined routes
All navigation has a beginning and an end, with points along the way. By designating routes that are clear and continuous, with well-defined landmarks, you've made a path that's easy to follow.

Provide help at decision points
Use point, line, and plane to identify key decision points along the route. Provide supporting signage in those critical spots. Make sure that signs are well within sight lines so that travelers can easily predict what lies ahead.

Create marked destinations
In both physical and virtual environments the user needs to know when they've arrived. This is easily communicated through signage, significant landmarks, color coding, etc.

Keep it simple
Too many signs equals too many choices, and too many choices equals confusion. When practicing wayfinding, cross-referencing the tenets of cognitive theories such as Miller's Magic Number (p. 60) and Information Overload (p. 75) will remind you to minimize the decisions your user has to make to reach the goal destination.

For more information about structuring content to enhance wayfinding, read the following sections of Chapter 5:
- *LATCH (Location, Alphabet, Time, Category, Hierarchy) Organization (p. 82)*
- *The Principle of Least Effort (p. 86)*
- *Uncertainty Reduction Theory (p. 88)*

For more information about design choices that enhance wayfinding, read the following section of Chapter 6:
- *Legibility (p. 108)*

Process

Information
Overload

American futurist and writer Alvin Toffler is credited with coining the term "information overload" in his 1970 book *Future Shock*, referring to an individual's inability to process, assimilate, and understand information due to the overwhelming amount of data available.[1]

1. Read about Toffler's theory of information overload in *Future Shock*, p. 350 (Bantam Books, 1970).

2. Wilson worked as a consultant for Hewlett-Packard to provide insight into the effects of communication technology in the modern workplace. This one-day study involved a survey of 1,000 people and an experiment with eight subjects.

3. Map shock has been documented by Dr. Donald F. Dansereau, Professor of Psychology at the Institute of Behavior Research at Texas Christian University.

4. For more about this phenomenon, read Richard Saul Wurman's books *Information Anxiety* (Bantam Books, 1990) and *Information Anxiety 2* (Que, 2000).

Theoretically, today's communication tools—combined with the rate at which new information is discovered and disseminated—compound the problem, leaving individuals unable to determine which information is relevant and credible. This can render them incapable of making decisions.

The term "information overload" is often used to describe contemporary work conditions, in which employees are bombarded with landline and mobile phone calls, e-mail, SMS texts, instant messaging, and noise pollution from the open cubicle environment. A study conducted by psychiatrist Glenn Wilson from King's College at the University of London, and sponsored by Hewlett-Packard, suggests that IQ levels may drop temporarily by as much as 10 points as modern office workers try to juggle a myriad communications.[2] The study points to e-mail as the largest contributor to this lack of concentration, stating that individuals feel compelled to answer each new message, perpetually changing their focus of attention and train of thought.

When information overload is created by graphic content, it is called "map shock." Map shock, also sometimes called visual shock, is a phenomenon experienced by individuals when encountering complex maps, diagrams, or pictorial representations. Information processing stops as the person tries to orient themselves to the overwhelming quantity of data. Users describe a sense of being lost, and of not knowing where to start, often accompanied by a physical, sometimes even audible, reaction.[3]

Information overload and map shock are concepts closely related, and perhaps even contributing factors, to "information anxiety," a term first used by Richard Saul Wurman in his book of the same name.[4] Wurman refers to information anxiety as "the black hole between data and knowledge," a condition created by exposure to massive amounts of information with no clarity of message. Individuals with information anxiety are stressed because they don't know how to process the data they're receiving, but they feel they should. It's an increasingly relevant phenomenon as internet access creates a culture of information seekers. A huge portion of the world's knowledge lies at our fingertips, but limited competencies in terms of comprehension and communication often block our access. The quantity, composition, and structure of information can influence motivation and concentration. Good design has the power to prevent poor user experiences and lost opportunities.

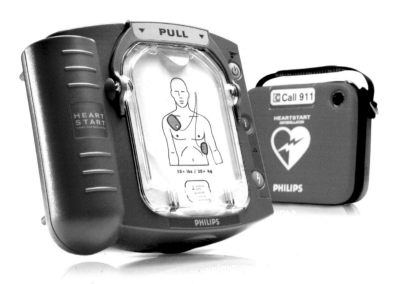

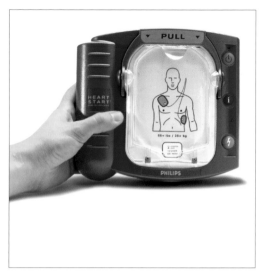

↗ ↗

The design of the Philips HeartStart home defibrillator is the perfect example of minimizing information overload through simple and elegant design. All the unfamiliar user has to do in an emergency situation is turn the device on, place the pads on the injured person's chest, and deliver a life-saving shock. Everything about the unit is designed to facilitate quick thinking and clear action.

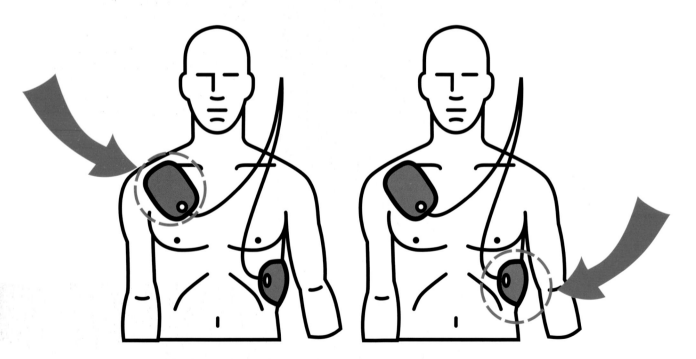

For more about how communication and aesthetic principles can help to prevent information overload, read the following sections of Chapters 5 and 6:

· *AIDA (Attention Interest Desire Action) (p. 80)*
· *LATCH (Location, Alphabet, Time, Category, Hierarchy) Organization (p. 82)*
· *Structure (p. 98)*
· *Legibility (p. 108)*

←
The simple yet effective illustrations placed on the pads of the Philips Heartstart ensure that proper positioning is universally understood.

Quick Tips

Don't decorate, design
Complex graphic presentations can feel overwhelming. Keep the design simple so that users feel comfortable. Focus on clarity by doing the minimum necessary to convey each idea. Avoid anything that doesn't serve a function (decorative flourishes, unnecessary gradients, meaningless patterns, etc.).

Provide options
Some people want to know all the details, others just require a general understanding. Structure information in ways that allow the reader to attain multiple levels of understanding, from overview to expert. Make sure that content and accessibility are centered on the unique needs of each individual user.

Use structure to create meaning
Designers don't always have a choice about how much information they are asked to organize. Awareness of the emotional and cognitive effects of information overload should influence aesthetic decisions. Use Miller's Magic Number (p. 60) to break information sets into visual chunks, creating more digestible "information bites."

Communication studies seek to understand how people transmit knowledge, share concepts, and process information through language.

The discipline can be directed at various topics and methods. Topics might be of economic, commercial, cultural, social, or political origin.

Practitioners often study a range of messaging delivery methods, including one-on-one discussions, group discussions, oratory, rhetoric, advertising, journalism, broadcast media, the internet, and even fictional representation through film and literature. Some of these delivery methods are relevant specifically to interpersonal communication and others focus on mass communication.

Interpersonal communication focuses on interactions between a pair of individuals, or groups of individuals; it concerns the relationships between sender and receiver, message and feedback. Mass communication is concerned with relaying information to broader populations, and the effect of media on message. Often the vehicle for distributing information—rather than content—determines whether the intended communication is interpersonal or mass. For example, in a retail setting, a sales pitch delivered by an employee to a potential customer is an example of interpersonal communication. If that same sales pitch is filmed and distributed via a television broadcast, in the form of a commercial, it becomes mass communication.

Feedback, or the response to a message, can be categorized as direct or indirect. Direct responses primarily come in the form of verbal communication (e.g. "I like you"). Indirect responses are often delivered through body language (e.g. blushing, smiling). During interpersonal communication, the sender can adapt the message based on the immediate feedback received from the audience. Conversely, in mass communication, the sender is often disssociated from the audience by time and physical location, and is thus unable to receive feedback in real time. Interpersonal communication, therefore, allows for a more tailored message than most mass communications. However, the advent of the internet has highlighted convergences between the tenets of interpersonal and mass communication, especially with regard to direct response time.

The study of communication is broad, continually evolving, and spans many disciplines. Designers can gain great insight by studying its tenets—indeed, many now refer to graphic development as "visual communication design." Numerous lessons from communication theory can be applied directly to information design projects, providing insight on message structuring, language use, and audience needs and expectations. In this chapter we'll explore some of these theories with a focus on organization, familiarity, and literacy.

The organization of content directly affects our ability to receive a message. If the information appears jumbled or overwhelming, many viewers "disconnect" before a transmission is completed. The following communication models and theories relate directly to the structure and accessibility of information.

AIDA (Attention, Interest, Desire, Action): A Persuasive Sales Model

Developed by E. St. Elmo Lewis, a pioneer of American advertising, AIDA is a model that describes the sales process.

In the late 1890s and early 1900s Lewis conducted research in person-to-person sales. He wanted to understand how effective salespeople led their customers to a buying decision. His investigations, based on intuition and observation, produced this formula:

· *Attention or awareness must be developed; the audience must be cognizant of the product or service.*

· *Interest must be generated so the audience learns more about the offering.*

· *Desire must be created, evoking an emotional response.*

· *Action will then be taken by the audience, eliciting the desired response.*

AIDA has been frequently adapted over the years, becoming the foundation for other marketing plans known as "hierarchy of effects models," in which customers move systematically through distinct phases to make purchasing decisions. AIDA and similar hierarchy of effects models have been used extensively in marketing, to help companies create more structured sales approaches; in business writing, to generate persuasive communications; and in advertising, to influence and gauge the effectiveness of campaigns.

While AIDA is primarily used as a sales tool, it can also provide insight for information designers on the structure, delivery, and acceptance of content, and is most successful when the needs of the customer or end user are fully understood. Individuals seek different kinds of information at various stages of the process. Grabbing a potential buyer's attention requires rapid messaging, but generating interest or evoking desire is often a much more complex process.

Consider a cookbook as an example. One text might simply list recipes, perhaps accompanied by photographs of the resulting dishes. Another volume might feature a written discussion of how the recipe was created, outlining the basic principles of the cuisine and its cooking techniques, accompanied by step-by-step illustrations as well as glossy photographs of the final meal; perhaps even the tools, ingredients, and cultural influences of the dish are examined. In either case, the reader's attention might be grabbed by a headline or a photo, or even the craving that first sent them looking for that particular book (mmmm... steak!). But in the latter example, the user has access to different kinds of information—and when carefully crafted, that content becomes a story that evokes both interest and desire. Whether the goal is selling more books, generating interest in cooking, or encouraging people to try a new cuisine, the tenets of good design combined with communication theories such as AIDA turn data sets into experiences.

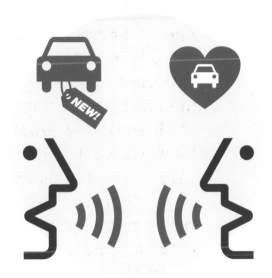

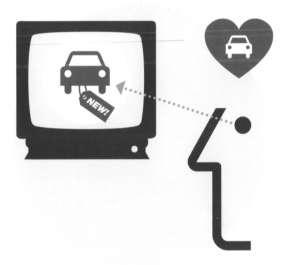

↗
The dialogue between a salesperson and a customer is an example of interpersonal communication. Feedback is instantaneous because each person can tailor their message to the reactions and response of the other. AIDA was created to define the successful person-to-person sales process.

↑
When a message is broadcast to a large audience it is considered to be mass communication. Feedback will be indirect because the recipients' reactions are not observed in real time. The sender may not know whether the message was acknowledged, understood, or even received. Feedback may take the form of written responses, telephone calls, or a rise (or drop) in sales. AIDA can also be adapted for mass communication.

Theories

Organization

1. The LATCH concept first appears in Wurman's book *Information Anxiety* as "The Five Hatracks," where the organizers are listed as Category, Time, Location, Alphabet, and Continuum. Wurman updates the idea in *Information Anxiety 2*, changing Continuum to Hierarchy and reordering to create the LATCH acronym.

2. TED (Technology, Entertainment, Design) began as a conference, created by Richard Saul Wurman in 1984, and has since become a global community dedicated to disseminating ideas. Two of the case studies in this book were presented at TED conferences—the Surplus and Debt film by Explanation Graphics (p. 178), and Jonathan Harris's interactive projects (p. 197). You can watch TED presentations online at www.ted.com, or download free podcasts via iTunes.

LATCH (Location, Alphabet, Time, Category, Hierarchy) Organization

LATCH[1] is a model for organizing information developed by Richard Saul Wurman—writer, designer, and founder of the popular TED (Technology, Entertainment, Design)[2] conferences, who is also famous for coining the term "information architect."

With LATCH, Wurman identifies just five ways to group content:

Location

Location structures information based on physical geography. Obvious examples are maps, transportation routes, and travel guides. Another example of organization by location occurs frequently in medical texts, where information is often grouped by location in the human body. Use location when physical connections are important to understanding.

Alphabet

Alphabetical organization bases content structure on letter sequence. This simple tool has proved very effective for numerous information artifacts, including dictionaries, encyclopedias, and telephone books. Use the alphabet when seeking a structure that will be broadly familiar to a diverse audience, or when placing very specific content (familiar or relevant to only a few) in a large pool of information.

Time

Frameworks based on time prove functional when users need to understand the sequence of events. Examples include calendars, arrival and departure boards for travel, cooking instructions, or timelines. Use time to structure content when users need to create schedules, or when the knowledge of a chain of events is highly relevant to the context.

Category

Categorical structures group information with similar features or attributes. Groupings may be broad or specific. E-commerce websites often group products by category (clothing, books, housewares), as do scientific classifications (flora and fauna). Organize data by category when you wish to enhance obvious connections between information sets.

Hierarchy

Hierarchy organizes information by measure (small to large, dark to light) or by perceived importance (rank, level, stature). Examples include food chains, emergency instructions, or military insignia. Use hierarchy to assign weight or value to the order of information.

Information designers must consider how the audience will locate and use content, determining which LATCH structure is most appropriate. Certain artifacts employ multiple structures. For example, most newspapers are divided into categories: a business section, a sports section, an arts section, etc. Within those individual sections, editors use hierarchy to place stories in order of perceived importance. The obituary section of the paper is organized alphabetically, because it is easiest to search by name. Box scores for most sporting events are listed in chronological order. And often weather is mapped by location. In this example, multiple structures provide a user-centered experience, allowing readers immediate access to their topic of choice and outlining information in the most accessible fashion relative to that topic.

Location	Alphabet	Time	Category	Hierarchy
Asia:	Canada	**Members Since 1945:**	**Permanent Members of the Security Council:**	**Percentage of Contribution to UN General Budget:**
China	China	Canada	China	United States (22%)
Japan	France	China	France	Japan (19.4%)
	Germany	Mexico	United Kingdom	Germany (8.6%)
Europe:	Italy	United Kingdom	United States	United Kingdom (6.1%)
France	Japan	United States		France (6%)
Germany	Mexico		**Elected Members of the Security Council (2008):**	Italy (4.8%)
Italy	Spain	**Members Since 1955:**	Italy	Canada (2.8%)
Spain	United Kingdom	Italy		Spain (2.5%)
United Kingdom	United States	Spain		China (2%)
			Not Currently Elected Members of the Security Council (2008):	Mexico (1.8%)
North America:		**Members Since 1956:**	Canada	
Canada		Japan	Germany	
United States		France	Japan	
South America:		**Members Since 1973:**		
Mexico		Germany		

←
According to Richard Saul Wurman's LATCH theory, there are only five ways to organize information: Location, Alphabet, Time, Category, and Hierarchy.

Here, LATCH is used to organize information about 10 United Nations member states.

←
The Vietnam Memorial Wall in Washington, DC, designed by artist Maya Lin, shows how organization can create or enhance meaning. The wall contains the names of more than 58,000 American servicemen and women who died or went missing during the Vietnam conflict. Instead of an alphabetical listing, as is common in obituary pages, or a hierarchical listing by military rank, these names appear chronologically by time of death or disappearance. Each individual is, in effect, surrounded by those who died with them. Using time to structure the list frames loss in a new way, often having a profound impact on those who visit the monument.

Inverted Pyramid Writing

The inverted pyramid style of writing is a common framework for journalism, and has been widely adopted by the web development community as the most effective structure for delivering written content online.

This style places the most important or newsworthy information at the beginning of the story, and orders the remaining information based on relative importance. Inverted pyramid copy starts with a lead, usually the first sentence or sometimes the first two sentences, which explains to the reader the most relevant and important information. Most leads are short and answer details about who, what, when, where, why, and how. Hard leads are concise statements that summarize the facts. Soft leads take a more narrative or creative approach, setting a scene in which to place those facts. Leads are followed by supporting information, and the story concludes with background and technical details.

The inverted pyramid takes its name from the structure of the content. The most important information is at the top, and supporting details are included in order of importance, allowing editors to cut quickly from the bottom up rather than restructuring the story entirely. Some historians postulate that this structure became widespread during the American Civil War as news stories were released over telegraph wires. Transmissions were expensive, usually priced per word, and connections were temperamental, often breaking before an entire news story could be sent. This technological influence forced editors and writers to convey the essence of their stories as quickly and succinctly as possible, but simultaneously allowed news to be shared in a more immediate fashion.

Time constraints, eye fatigue, and the short attention spans of online readers make inverted pyramid writing ideal for websites. The structure ensures that readers will process the core message even if they don't finish reading the entire article—which suits a skim-and-scan culture perfectly. Though the inverted pyramid was designed for written messaging, its organizational structure can easily be applied to visual communication projects, using aesthetics to implement the hierarchy of information.

Lead (who, what, where, when, why, how)

Supporting Information

Details

For information on how communication structures can benefit from cognitive theory, read these sections of Chapter 4:
- *Memory (p. 58)*
- *Wayfinding (p. 72)*
- *Information Overload (p. 75)*

For information on how organization can be affected by aesthetic decisions, read these sections of Chapter 6:
- *Hierarchy (p. 105)*
- *Color (p. 108)*
- *Typography (p. 120)*

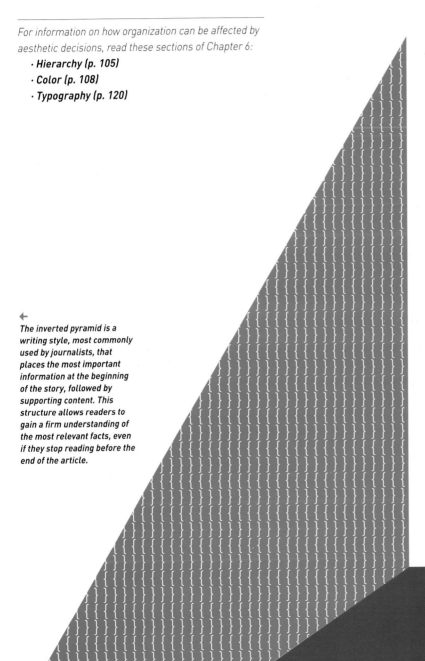

←
The inverted pyramid is a writing style, most commonly used by journalists, that places the most important information at the beginning of the story, followed by supporting content. This structure allows readers to gain a firm understanding of the most relevant facts, even if they stop reading before the end of the article.

Quick Tips

Tell me a story
When appropriate, use stories or anecdotes to place information in context. This makes your message easier to understand and relate to, and creates an emotional connection with the audience that they will remember.

I've done this before
For each unique assignment, consider how the end user might prefer to access content. Has a precedent already been set (e.g. dictionaries are arranged alphabetically)? Carefully consider whether changes you might make to organization would help or hinder the communication of the message. Often, instead of switching to a completely new structure, you can employ more than one to meet the needs of multiple users.

Just the facts
When you have limited time to communicate a message, stick to the facts. Using the concept of the inverted pyramid to structure design enables the viewer to grab the core message quickly. Develop typographic systems that clearly frame content and enhance skimming and scanning.

Theories

Familiarity

Our capacity for learning is often linked with our emotional state. Frustration and confusion certainly make for a less receptive audience. Prepare a path for your message by first setting your user at ease.

The Principle of Least Effort

In Library and Information Science studies, the Principle of Least Effort[1] describes the searching and seeking behavior of users.

The theory was developed by Thomas Mann, a general reference librarian at the US Library of Congress (the largest library in the world). It states that regardless of experience and expertise, users will naturally gravitate to familiar and easy tools, even if the resulting yield is poor. According to Mann, "Most researchers (even serious scholars) will tend to choose easily available information sources, even when they are of objectively low quality, in preference to pursuing higher-quality sources whose use would require a greater expenditure of effort."[2] This theory describes our natural proclivity to utilize tools that are simple, accessible, familiar, and comfortable. As explained by Mann, ease of use may be more important to the researcher than the quality of results they find.

Mann has written about the Principle of Least Effort not in an effort to malign researchers, but rather to illuminate potential flaws in the design of library systems and search options. He stresses that it is poor practice to blame the

1. Note that the term "Principle of Least Effort" has been used before by other theorists to describe human behavior. Particularly influential is George Zipf's *Human Behavior and the Principle of Least Effort* (Addison-Wesley Publishing Co. Inc, 1949).

2. You can find this quote, along with more about the information-seeking habits of library patrons, on p. 91 of Mann's book *Library Research Models: A Guide to Classification, Cataloging, and Computers* (Oxford University Press, USA, 1993).

"lazy user" without evaluating the design they are having difficulty navigating.

The study of information-seeking habits within a library, whether physical or virtual, provides a very useful analogy for visual communication designers. We can learn from Mann's Principle of Least Effort when considering how our audiences search the content of the artifacts we create: from wayfinding in physical spaces (Where is the bathroom?), to the organization of an e-commerce site (How do I check out?), to the structure of a travel guide (How do I get to that restaurant from my hotel?). At the start of every information design undertaking, the end user's needs should be the primary focus. Forecasting their abilities, tools of choice, familiarity with technology, access to media, and so on, will help the design team to determine the appropriate artifact and information structure for clear communication. Combined with germane aesthetics, the message not only gets through, it is memorable.

The Principle of Least Effort states that researchers will accept results from the most accessible source, such as the internet—even when better information could be found at the library, or by examining archives.

Theories

Familiarity

1. The Uncertainty Reduction Theory was first presented by Charles Berger and Richard Calabrese in their 1975 paper "Some Exploration in Initial Interaction and Beyond: Toward a Developmental Theory of Communication" in the journal *Human Communication Research*. You can find a complete list of related axioms and theorems in that article.

Uncertainty Reduction Theory

The Uncertainty Reduction Theory[1] is an interpersonal communication principle that provides insight into social interaction, defining how individuals cope when meeting strangers.

The basic premise of the theory is simple: uncertainty is unpleasant, so we use language and communication to reduce it. The theory postulates that when encountering a new person, or group of people, we move through three different phases of discovery: Entry, Personal, and Exit. The end goal of this process is to build a level of understanding so that we can more easily predict behavior, thereby reducing uncertainty and discomfort.

In the Entry phase, communication is regulated by commonly accepted social rules. People may shake hands or engage in other customary nonverbal greetings; introduce themselves in either a casual or a formal fashion; or engage in polite generalities of conversation, such as "The weather's great today!" or "How about that local sports team?" The Personal phase begins when the engaged parties begin to feel relaxed and start to share information more freely. The exchange of dialogue in the Personal phase will allude to beliefs and values without addressing any contentious issues. Questions posed in this phase might be like this: "Where do you work?" or "What kind of music do you listen to?" At this point conversations may seem to flow more easily. The last step, called the Exit phase, is where negotiations determine whether the relationship will continue or conclude: "May I have your business card?" or "It was nice to meet you."

Though the Uncertainty Reduction Theory is centered around interpersonal exchanges, some of the axioms it presents apply equally to visual communication. These are paraphrased here:

· *When we are uncertain, we actively seek information.*

· *Certainty is enhanced by similarities, and minimized by differences.*

· *That of which we are uncertain becomes less favorable.*

Apply these concepts to your next information design project. When delivering new or unfamiliar content, consider those factors that might help reduce uncertainty and influence your end user to actively receive and process knowledge.

→

The Uncertainty Reduction Theory provides insight into social interaction, defining how individuals cope when meeting strangers. The theory outlines three phases—Entry, Personal, and Exit—during which each person engages in information-seeking strategies to reduce uncertainty and form opinions about the other.

Entry

Personal

Exit

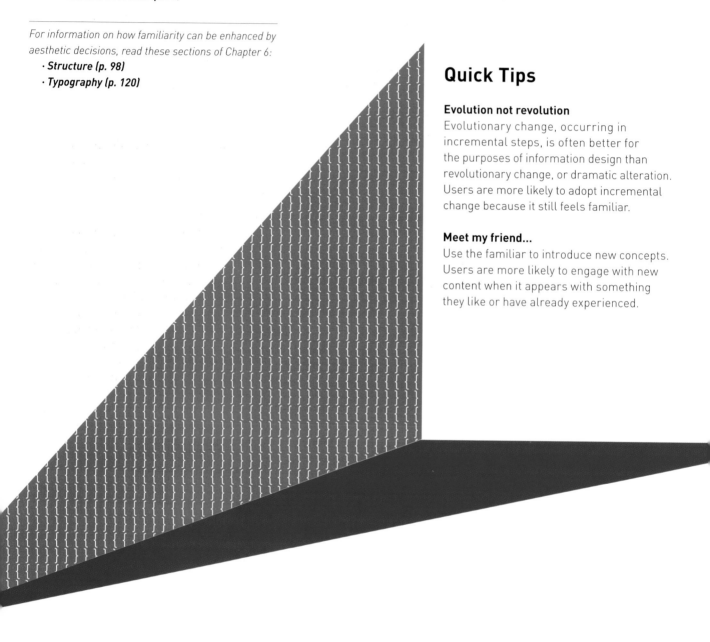

For information on how familiarity is connected to cognition, read these theories in Chapter 4:

- **The Stage Theory Model (p. 58)**
- **Eye Tracking (p. 66)**
- **Wayfinding (p. 72)**
- **Information Overload (p. 75)**

For information on how familiarity can be enhanced by aesthetic decisions, read these sections of Chapter 6:

- **Structure (p. 98)**
- **Typography (p. 120)**

Quick Tips

Evolution not revolution
Evolutionary change, occurring in incremental steps, is often better for the purposes of information design than revolutionary change, or dramatic alteration. Users are more likely to adopt incremental change because it still feels familiar.

Meet my friend...
Use the familiar to introduce new concepts. Users are more likely to engage with new content when it appears with something they like or have already experienced.

Literacy issues are of utmost importance to information designers because they affect the audience's ability to receive messages. In a knowledge economy, our understanding of the term "literacy" has expanded. It no longer simply refers to reading and writing skills, but also focuses on the ability to find, process, interpret, and apply information. The following three fields of study form a foundation for modern communicators.

Information Literacy

Information literacy describes an individual's ability to recognize when information is needed, and then have the skills to find, evaluate, analyze, and effectively use that information.

Information-literate individuals are able to efficiently identify legitimate information resources and filter out sources of questionable integrity.

Visual Literacy

Visual literacy is an essential component of information literacy. Visual literacy focuses on our ability to interpret, appreciate, gather, and create images. These images can aid thinking, clarify decision making, enhance learning, and strengthen communication. Computer technology has empowered the everyday user with the ability to rapidly generate visual displays of information, so charts and graphs are more commonplace than ever before, and supporting imagery accompanies almost every presentation, from elementary schools to boardrooms. Audiences must realize that not all images are objective and that many are altered—some accidentally, and others for manipulative purposes. In a culture where the influence of the internet, film, and television is far exceeding that of the printed word, visual literacy and critical analysis are more vital than ever.

← Information literacy describes the ability to locate, evaluate, and apply information, while distinguishing between legitimate and questionable sources.

← Visual literacy describes the ability to appreciate, analyze, create, and utilize visuals for communication and learning.

Semiotics

Semiotics, the study of signs and symbols as elements of language and communication, informs our ability to interpret images or other sensory input. Semiotics strives to understand and explain how different meanings are assigned, based on variables of sender, receiver, context, and culture.

Central to semiotics is the concept of the "sign," defined as a word, image, sound, gesture, or any other sensory experience. Each sign possesses a "denotation," its most commonly accepted meaning, and often several "connotations," which are secondary associations based on an individual's personal experience. For example, an image of a skull and crossbones is immediately associated with death (denotation), but can also conjure thoughts of pirates, secret societies, poison, or even retail clothing lines (connotations). Individual signs are further classified as icons, symbols, or indexes:

Icons are literal visual representations. For example, a drawing of a car looks like an actual car.

Symbols are more abstract and may represent things that don't have physical form. For example, the international symbol for "biohazard" is an abstracted series of circles.

Indexes create connections between objects, using that which is easy to describe to identify something more obscure. For example, the image of an umbrella is used to indicate wet weather.

Context, culture, and personal experience influence a sign's denotation and connotations. But those influences are not fixed. As our experiences evolve, so does the meaning we ascribe to signs. The skull and crossbones that once adorned Jolly Roger flags struck fear into the hearts of mariners—often literally meaning "death is approaching." Today you can find the same symbol on T-shirts, neckties, shoes, and even baby clothes. The level of fear associated with the symbol has been diminished by popular culture and merchandising. Consider, too, how radically context can change a sign's meaning: a skull and crossbones placed on a bottle indicates poison, whereas on a necktie it might instead imply a nonconformist fashion ideal. Whether the popularization of the skull and crossbones in fashion will dilute the symbol's ability to communicate danger to future generations remains to be seen.

Communication is never static. Information designers must earnestly consider how cultural and contextual associations will affect the end user's interpretation of a message.

↑
Signs can be classified as icons, symbols, or indexes.

Icon = literal visual representation

Symbol = abstract representation

Index = representation by connection

Shown here:
The icon for taxi

The internationally recognized symbol meaning "biohazard"

An indexical representation of rain

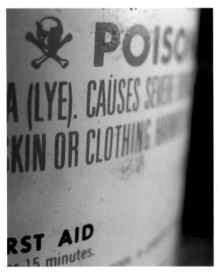

↑
Semiotic signs have denotations and connotations. A denotation is the primary, culturally accepted meaning. Connotations are secondary, associated meanings, based on an individual's personal experiences. Take this image of a skull and crossbones as an example. The denotation is death. Connotations might include poison, toxicity, pirates, secret societies, counterculture fashion, etc.

→
Even icons age. This mark, used to indicate a telephone, is based on the literal depiction of a rotary dial phone—which has not been in production for 20 years. This icon may not communicate to future generations who have never encountered the original artifact.

For more information on how cognitive processes affect literacy, read these theories in Chapter 4:
- **The Stage Theory Model (p. 58)**
- **Information Overload (p. 75)**

For more information on how aesthetic decisions affect literacy, read these sections of Chapter 6:
- **Structure (p. 98)**
- **Color (p. 108)**

Quick Tips

Don't reinvent the wheel

Use customary icons and symbols to ensure unequivocal communication. If your audience is already familiar with a sign, use it. Don't waste time or sacrifice clarity for style.

Does this mean something to you?

Be aware of cultural changes to ensure that symbols and icons consistently communicate their message to a broad audience. For example, the common sign for "telephone" is an iconic representation of a rotary dial unit, which has not been in production for more than two decades. Younger audiences and future generations will be less likely to recognize this icon because of their lack of exposure to the original artifact.

Native language

When designing for a foreign market you need to become familiar with the visual language of your audience. For example, some audiences prefer photographic imagery to iconography or typography. A literature review or ethnographic study can help determine these preferences.

Historically, the designer's primary concern has been the visual presentation of a message.

In the modern marketplace, the emergence of the designer as author, business person, consultant, and thought leader has significantly augmented those traditional aesthetic skills.

However, our roots remain visual. Can we assign new value to those terms and tenets learned in the art-school classroom? Beyond beauty, what communication merits are apparent in the study of alignment, hierarchy, spatial placement, contrast, color theory, and typography?

A clear explanation of aesthetic decisions—framed by logic, supported by visual standards, and imbued with creative enthusiasm—assures design buyers that their money has been well spent. Better still, the appropriate application of these principles connects the audience with the intended message.

For the purposes of information design studies, most aesthetic principles can be organized into two overlapping categories: structure and legibility.

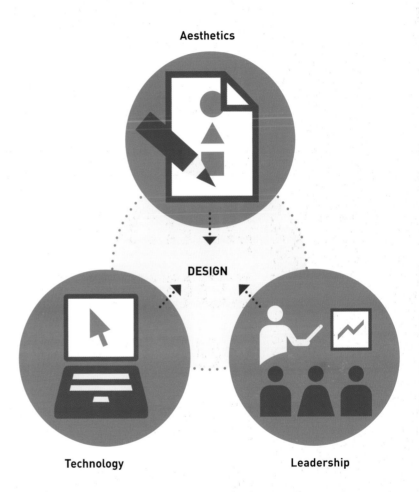

Aesthetics

DESIGN

Technology

Leadership

Traditional aesthetic and creative skills, combined with advanced technical competency and the ability to be a thought leader, from classroom to community to corporation, provide a firm foundation for the modern designer.

Designers use grids to organize content and manage the clarity of a message.

Newspapers, magazines, and periodicals are an obvious example due to their typographic grid systems, but grids can be applied to most print, digital, and even three-dimensional work. When you start looking you'll find them almost everywhere.

One of the initial focuses of a design education is learning to organize content and create hierarchy by using grid systems. After creative and conceptual development, the layout of the grid—ratios, number of columns, width of gutters and margins, horizontal and vertical relationships—is often the first aesthetic undertaking, one that will greatly affect the final look, feel, and usability of a design piece. For some students the grid can feel claustrophobic, limiting choices and restricting artistic license. But that reaction reflects a misunderstanding of the device.

With more practice—and with tight deadlines and copious information sets to juggle—the grid reveals itself as integral, and perhaps even inspirational: a foundation for order, an agent of clarity.

From an information design perspective, grids provide a canvas for content. A grid is an essential aesthetic device that will allow the designer to walk the reader through that content, one specific message at a time, without actually being there. Grid systems allow the designer to create visual clarity through organization, movement, and grouping.

Grid Divisions

Grids are used to organize content in every type of media.

The circular grid on this card provides a frame for content, ensuring that it will consistently appear through the die-cut window above.

This website uses clear structural alignments to control complex amounts of content, creating a positive online user experience.

Here the grid is used in an environmental setting to provide a tapestry of imagery.

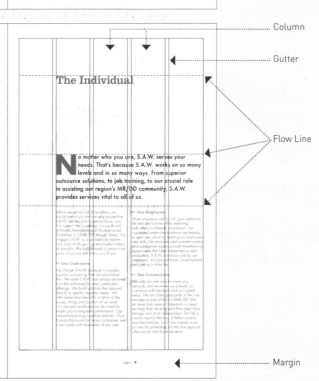

← ↖
Basic grid structures include margins, columns, and gutters. Adding horizontal lines provides additional visual continuity. The most common horizontal inclusion is a "hanging line" or "flow line" from which headlines, quotations, or body copy can flow. Grids allow the designer to easily delineate segments of the layout for specific content.

The Individual

No matter who you are, S.A.W. serves your needs. That's because S.A.W. works on so many levels and in so many ways. From superior outsource solutions, to job training, to our crucial role in assisting our region's MR/DD community, S.A.W. provides services vital to all of us.

Column

Gutter

Flow Line

Margin

Organization

The geometric divisions of a grid create a framework for typographic and pictorial content. On a micro level, they provide consistency on a single page; on a macro level, they do the same across chapters, volumes, or entire websites. Consistency is extremely important to usability. Viewers can process content more rapidly when they are familiar with the structure of information. Imagine the difficulty of traversing a website where the navigation was constantly moving, or speed-reading a paperback novel if the paragraph width changed dramatically from page to page. The organizational qualities of a grid provide easy and consistent access to content.

→

Repeating organizational structures (common grids, alignments, hanging lines, etc.) increases usability by providing the viewer with predictable formats for retrieving content. This website for Reich Paper provides users with a consistent viewing experience, focusing their attention on the information and not the interface with harmonious and familiar typographic, interactive, and wayfinding systems.

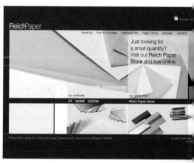

Movement

Direct and implied alignments on the grid provide links between information sets and move the viewer's eye through the content of the page. Depending on the complexity of the layout, that movement may affect how long a reader remains engaged with a design piece. By using grid alignments and spacing choices to compartmentalize information sets, the designer can control large quantities of content. By controlling how the reader's eye moves through that content, the grid can also impart a sense of time or show direction. Considering eye movement and rhythm when working with a grid enhances the skimming and scanning of information, helping the viewer to locate relevant content quickly.

↗ →
Designers use grids to create dynamic movement on the page, convey a sense of space, and establish relationships between information sets. Consider how your eye moves around the three layouts shown here, all with the same amount of content on a common four-column grid.

Grouping

In addition to providing a means of organization, grids allow the designer to connect groups of content by placing them in proximity and alignment with one another. Arranging information sets in this way creates new contexts and can suggest different meanings than if the sets were reviewed independently. Proximity and placement lead the viewer to believe that the items in the grouped information sets are related. For example, a paragraph about declining coral populations might be a part of a zoological study on the reproductive habits of polyp colonies, but when placed alongside a satellite photograph of melting icecaps and an annual temperature index, the grouping immediately evokes the topic of global warming. Visual communicators should be aware of this and ensure that the design always delivers the intended message.

↗ →

Placement, proximity, and similarity can dramatically change the context of content. In this example, our emotional response to the dog image changes dramatically when it is placed with an image of a young family or converted to grayscale and paired with a photograph of a cage.

Quick Tips

Borrow from the familiar

Not sure where to start when designing a grid? Use the Golden Ratio (also known as Golden or Divine Proportions) to determine page margins—the ratio of the longer part to the whole should be the same as the ratio of the shorter part to the longer part. The Golden Ratio is present in nature, art, and architecture, and thus creates a structure with which your viewer will immediately feel familiar.

Look both ways

In addition to vertical columns, horizontal flowlines (implied alignments or actual linear elements from which body copy or other content consistently hangs) and a baseline grid (horizontal alignments between type sets) create a more consistent viewing experience.

For web work, think proportionally

When designing for the web, don't think of columns in terms of fixed width, because webpages are resized according to browser width and viewer preference. Concentrate instead on creating structural value by focusing on proportional relations between page elements (based on ems). Essentially, the user sets the scale and your design expands to fit.

For more information on how grids work from a cognitive perspective, read these theories in Chapter 4:
- **The Gestalt Principles of Perception (p. 64)**
- **Eye Tracking (p. 66)**

For more information on how grids support communication paradigms, read these theories in Chapter 5:
- **The Principle of Least Effort (p. 86)**
- **Uncertainty Reduction Theory (p. 88)**

In the context of graphic design, "hierarchy" refers to the ordering of pictorial and typographic information sets so that the viewer can quickly gain an understanding of their relative importance.

The user's comprehension of an informational hierarchy requires two processes: first, a quick grab or overview; and second, a more detailed consumption of the content. In the quick-grab stage, the user is searching for the fundamental message, and average attention spans dictate that there are only seconds for them to find it. The use of color, anomaly, dramatic contrast, and positioning can all affect the focal point of a design piece. That focal point, the first thing that really catches the viewer's eye, strongly influences their overview of the message. As readers proceed through levels of information (body copy, captions, footnotes, supporting charts and graphs, etc.), they process how that content supports the core message. During the detailed consumption phase, typographic differentiation, grid structures and consistent alignments, principles of contrast, and color coding can help the reader connect and rank information sets.

Graphic and informational hierarchy should be apparent in every design piece, but are especially important for complex information design projects. In these cases, using aesthetic principles to create a clear hierarchy leads the user through complex content in a way that is both logical and accessible. It also alleviates phenomena like map shock and information overload (see p. 75), instead turning overwhelming streams of data into a positive learning experience.

Designers need to understand their core content so that the hierarchical systems they create support and reinforce the message. Sometimes, altering the order of information can affect its meaning. It is imperative to examine hierarchy throughout the various phases of design development.

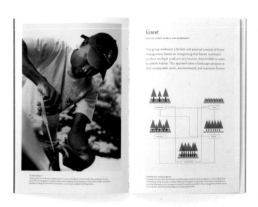

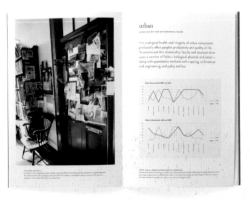

Southern Connecticut serves as a classroom for urban and restoration ecology. Several rivers enter Long Island Sound in New Haven, and nearby university research sites include the 7,800-acre Yale-Myers Forest. On one-day trips and during summer-long projects, students find many varied opportunities to study ecology without going far afield.

ecology

ECOLOGY, ECOSYSTEMS, AND BIODIVERSITY

This group's aim is to understand the complex interrelationships between humans and the diverse organisms living in ecosystems. Faculty and student members study how organisms interact with one another and with their physical and chemical environments, and they analyze the causes of changes in global species distribution and abundance. They do so by integrating chemistry and biology, biophysics, physiology, genetics, evolution, mathematical modeling, and the social sciences.

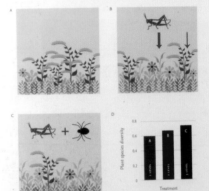

FOOD WEBS AND BIODIVERSITY
Experimental research examines the effect of top predators in maintaining plant species diversity. (A) A goldenrod species should dominate, yielding low diversity. (B) Grasshoppers prefer grasses (thick arrow) but will eat herb species, including goldenrod (thin arrow), reducing its dominance. (C) Scary spider predators cause grasshoppers to stop eating grass and to hide in and forage on goldenrod, leading to highest plant species diversity (D).

← ↑
Clear visual hierarchy is fundamental to graphic communication. It allows readers to skim and scan large fields of content and determine what is useful, usable, and relevant to their needs without having to read each and every word. These spreads from the Yale School of Forestry and Environmental Studies viewbook are excellent examples of visual hierarchy at work. They clearly direct the viewer to pertinent information sets, making the navigation of sometimes complex content quick and easy.

For related information on how users process complex information sets, read these theories in Chapter 4:
- **Perception of Graphic Statistical Displays: Cleveland's Task Model (p. 68)**
- **Miller's Magic Number (p. 60)**
- **Information Overload (p. 75)**

For more information on how visual hierarchy connects to communication paradigms, read these theories in Chapter 5:
- **LATCH (Location, Alphabet, Time, Category, Hierarchy) Organization (p. 82)**
- **The Principle of Least Effort (p. 86)**
- **Information Literacy (p. 91)**

Quick Tips

Reading is fundamental

Start a design project by familiarizing yourself with the core content. This will help you rank the information sets that need to be presented before you even start sketching. Don't forget to consider graphic elements that are features of the medium in which you're working (page numbers, common navigational elements, etc.).

Bigger isn't always better

To continually engage your viewer, explore different ways to create hierarchy. Employ color, spacing, position, or other graphic devices to create that initial focal point.

Most designers are enamored with color. Sure, a select few stick firmly to modernist themes of white, black, and red in their work, or hold forced allegiance to a corporate style manual's limited palette—but enter studios and homes and you'll likely find a cacophony of hues.

1. For a clear explanation of color blindness for the layperson, read "Can You Tell Red from Green?" by Dr. Alex Wade, available at the Vischeck website: http://www.vischeck.com/info/wade.php

Our art-school experiences have trained us well. We daydream about color pairings in the shower, can instantly produce the number of our favorite Pantone chip when asked, and organize our closets by tone.

We're well versed in technical and production issues related to color, too. Web designers consider variances between the way different monitors and platforms display color, and how luminosity affects color pairings. Print designers adjust for the way paper will absorb ink, how ink changes based on the hue of the stock on which it's printed, how saturation and value change from coated to uncoated stocks, and how varnishes affect tone. This industry-specific knowledge, focused on the production of our craft, is invaluable.

However, if information design is to focus on the needs of the end user, a thorough understanding of the audience's perception of color is also necessary. Physical, environmental, and cultural influences affect the way we see and interpret color.

→ *This interactive wall display at the Nobel Peace Center in Oslo, Norway, uses color to clearly delineate information about Nobel Laureates, helping visitors engage with each award winner's personal history.*

Physical Considerations

Visual Deficiencies

Perfect vision is a rare thing. Deficiencies are evident in every audience, market, and country. Perhaps you are wearing glasses as you read this text? Our eyes grow with our bodies and the sight of a child may be very different from that of her grandparents. Congenital or hereditary vision problems and the effects of age and environment all affect our perception of color. While no designer can forecast the visual vicissitudes of each individual audience member, general evaluations of a group's ocular abilities and requirements can influence design decisions.

Aging Eyes

It's no secret that our vision deteriorates as we grow older. Most estimates begin the descent in middle age—our forties and fifties. The aging or elderly eye may experience difficulty in low-light situations, and with differentiation of color.

Color Blindness

It is roughly estimated that one in 20 individuals will exhibit some kind of color-vision deficiency. The term "color blind" generally indicates a difficulty distinguishing between red and green, rather than a complete inability to perceive color. Men exhibit color blindness with a much greater frequency than women. Our bodies are always adapting, and thus individuals with color blindness often differentiate shapes instead of hues. This may make them better at finding objects in monochromatic settings, or making distinctions in camouflage.[1]

Original Image

Protanope Simulation

Dueteranope Simulation

Tritanope Simulation

→ *Websites like vischeck.com allow designers to upload images or web designs to determine how the work may appear to the visually impaired. Here, three common types of color blindness have been simulated.*

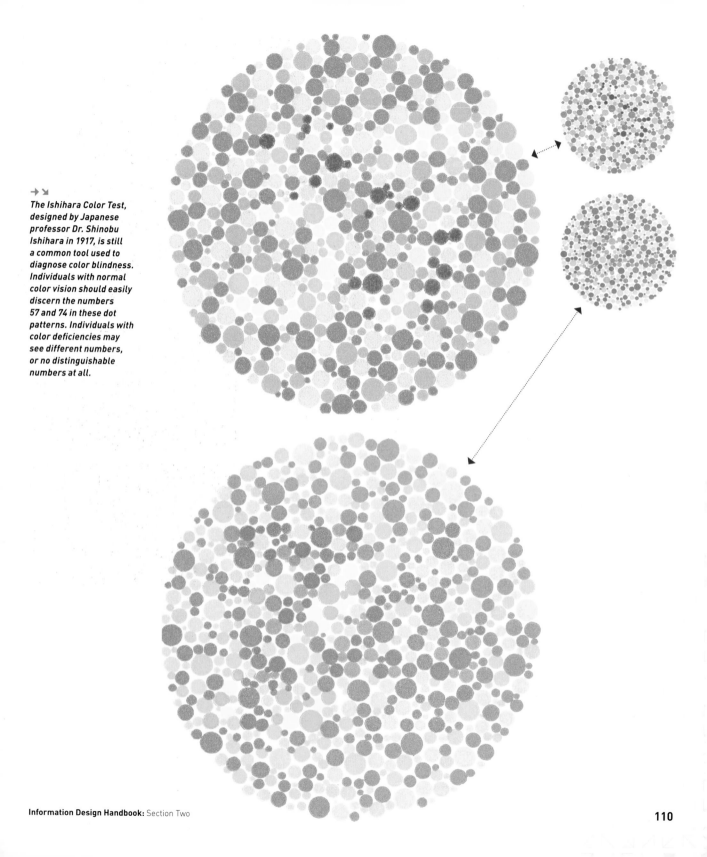

The Ishihara Color Test, designed by Japanese professor Dr. Shinobu Ishihara in 1917, is still a common tool used to diagnose color blindness. Individuals with normal color vision should easily discern the numbers 57 and 74 in these dot patterns. Individuals with color deficiencies may see different numbers, or no distinguishable numbers at all.

Typography and Older Viewers

by Paul J. Nini, Professor of Design,
The Ohio State University

Thirteen percent of the population [of the United States] is currently over 65 years old. In 30 years that group will double to 66 million people. People change as they age. Sensory, cognitive, and motor abilities decline. Graphic and visual communication designers may soon find themselves routinely creating information that must meet the needs of older viewers.

The main premise behind Universal or Inclusive Design is that by designing for those with the lowest ability, we ensure that everyone can easily use the results of our work. In the case of choosing appropriate typefaces for use with the aging eye, it is best to follow the ADA (Americans with Disabilities Act) guidelines on this subject. These standards ensure that more uniform typefaces are used, and that overly thick or thin stroke widths, and overly condensed (thin) or expanded (wide) letter proportions are not used.

Sans-serif styles tend to work best—as opposed to serif styles, which often have very thin areas within the letterforms. It's also very important that there be good visual contrast between the actual type and the surface on which it appears. Finally, the larger the type size the better, as testing designed for communications with older viewers routinely reveals.

↑ → ↘
As we grow older, we begin to lose the ability to differentiate color clearly, and many people suffer from a loss of ocular focus. This airport sign accounts for those visual deficiencies by employing dynamic contrast of hue and value, and by using an appropriately legible font. These images approximate various levels of ocular degeneration.

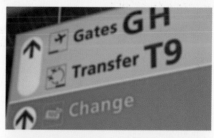

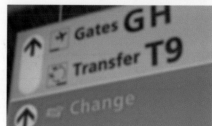

For a more detailed discussion of design decisions for older audiences, read Professor Nini's article "Typography and the Aging Eye: Typeface Legibility for Older Viewers with Vision Problems" at http://www.aiga.org/content.cfm/typography-and-the-aging-eye

Environmental Change

Lighting can have a dramatic effect on the perception of color—you've probably encountered this when altering the paint color on the walls of your home. There are, literally, day and night differences (natural lighting versus artificial lighting). When color is flooded with light it will appear washed out, and when it is poorly lit the same hue appears much darker. Natural light changes tone based on the sun's position in the sky and any exterior objects through which it might be filtered (consider the change in daylight when seen through the leaves of a tree). Artificial lighting can vary widely, too. Numerous options are available for specific energy consumption, illumination, and color-casting needs. It is imperative that designers spend time contemplating where, when, and how their work will be viewed. The details of lighting are especially influential on environmental design projects.

Atmospheric changes can also have a significant impact on color perception. Consider your own experiences trying to read road signs in heavy rain, snow, or fog. When designing for projects that will directly encounter the elements, or low-light/low-visibility situations, be sure to combine color and contrast for the greatest effect.

Color and contrast help us immediately recognize a change in our physical environment, or indicate importance in an interface. Dramatically contrasting stripes are often used to mark edges or stairs in industrial spaces. Color coding of emergency levers, buttons, and switches helps workers to act quickly in crisis situations. Color may well be the fastest way to convey a simple message.

Color		Meaning	Application
Safety Red PMS 1797 C		*Stop, Danger*	Signifies fire protection equipment, "danger," and "stop."
Safety Orange PMS 165 C		*Warning*	Signifies dangerous parts of machinery or electrical components which can crush, cut, or shock.
Safety Yellow PMS 124 C		*Caution*	Signifies physical hazards created by non-moving objects which can be fallen over or into, struck against, or between which one may be caught.
Safety Green PMS 341 C		*Safety*	Signifies areas and equipment associated with First Aid.
Safety Blue PMS 287 C		*Information*	Signifies safety information; used on informational signs and bulletin boards.
Black + White Process Black		*Boundaries*	Signifies housekeeping and traffic areas.
Safety Purple PMS Purple C		*Radiation*	Signifies x-ray, alpha, beta, gamma, neutron, and proton radiation.

↑
The US Department of Labor's Occupational Safety & Health Administration (OSHA) has produced guidelines for color-coding work environments. In this chart, each color is listed alongside its meaning and workplace application. For example, red indicates danger and should be used for emergency stop buttons on machinery.

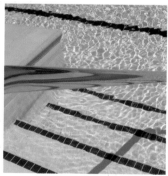

↑
Some emergency vehicles in the United Kingdom use bright yellow and green checkered patterns to ensure visibility in low light and foggy conditions. When compared with the use of red, a

common color for emergency vehicles in the US, visibility contrasts are striking. Many optometrists have noted lime green as a highly visible color, and suggest its use in emergency scenarios.

↑
Color is often used in the workplace as a quick indicator of different functions. Universal color coding on emergency buttons creates safer working conditions.

↑
In many environments, marking edges and boundaries with contrasting colors can help to ensure safety.

Cultural Considerations

Our interpretations of a color's meaning are highly influenced by culture. Numerous influences mold these interpretations, from religion to politics, linguistics to popular trends. Bridal dresses and mourning colors vary dramatically between cultures. Red and blue, when mentioned in unison, are instantly associated with politics in the United States. The Chinese celebrate the arrival of a baby girl with blue. In Islamic cultures, green is associated with paradise. In the United States, that same hue is the color of money, environmental movements, and low-calorie food.

For clear communication and unambiguous information delivery, it is essential to understand the needs, customs, and attitudes of the end user. Therefore, investigations into cultural perceptions of color are essential whenever designing for a new audience, market, or global campaign.

↗→

In many western cultures, white is the color most commonly associated with bridal gowns, but Indian brides are traditionally clothed in red. Colors carry different meanings across cultures, nations, and traditions. Be sure to have a clear understanding of your audience before making color selections.

Quick Tips

70 is the magic number

When designing with color, dramatic contrasts in hue and value, saturation, and brightness make for the most legible message. This simple rule addresses a great many vision problems, from aging to color blindness. The Americans with Disabilities Act (ADA) best practice suggests a 70 percent contrast between an object (type or icon) and its background.[2]

Test your assumptions

The World Wide Web Consortium (W3C) has utilized international standards to create color brightness and difference tests that help designers and developers determine whether RGB and hexadecimal color pairings maximize contrast for ease of viewing. Online color-contrast calculators utilize the W3C standards for almost instantaneous analysis of color pairings. Check out a particularly helpful example at: http://snook.ca/technical/colour_contrast/colour.html

Don't fade away

When designing for outdoor or light-saturated spaces, be sure to consult your fabricator regarding the environmental effects on materials and color retention.

You say "tomato," I say "red"

Keep in mind that perceptions of color are often highly individual. Physically, we all have different numbers of rods and cones in our eyes that may affect color recognition. Psychologically, we know best what we use most, so an audience of fashion designers or artists may immediately differentiate between subtle color differences like plum, violet, and indigo, where a group of investment bankers will see only purple.

Avoid eye strain

For information design purposes, avoid simultaneous-contrast color pairings that create a visual vibration when viewed together, and also combine to distort hue. Simultaneous contrast is most intense when the colors paired are complementary and of the same approximate value (see pp. 116–7).

For more information on how color functions from a cognitive perspective, read these theories in Chapter 4:
  · *The Gestalt Principles of Perception (p. 64)*
  · *Difference Threshold (p. 62)*

For more information on how color connects to communication paradigms, read these theories in Chapter 5:
  · *AIDA (Attention, Interest, Desire, Action) (p. 80)*
  · *LATCH (Location, Alphabet, Time, Category, Hierarchy) Organization (p. 82)*
  · *Information Literacy (p. 91)*

2. The Society for Environmental Graphic Designers (SEGD) provides white papers, courses, and publications that make the ADA guidelines easier for designers to understand. For more information, go to http://segd.org/

Contrast, or the study of visual oppositions, is easy to comprehend: light versus dark, small versus large, geometric versus organic—the options seem almost endless.

Contrast is to design what salt is to cooking. Layouts are simply dull without it (and too much makes them unpalatable). But beyond qualitative statements, contrast can greatly influence the legibility of a design piece. Contrast has a direct influence on the effectiveness of all the interrelated principles discussed in this chapter. The use of contrast to control information utilizes the human ability to see patterns, notice differences, and fixate on anomalies. These components of perception and cognition can be manipulated to help the information designer create structure, control hierarchy, sequence information, and ultimately create meaning.

Listed here are the most common ways to create visual contrast:

Color
There are a number of ways to achieve contrast with color:

Contrast in Hue
Position on the color wheel can help to determine the degree of contrast between two colors—the more distance that separates them on the color wheel, the more contrast there will be. Complementary colors—those opposite each other on the color wheel—provide the greatest contrast. Analogous colors—those located next to each other on the color wheel—provide the least.

Contrast in Value
Contrast also depends on the relative lightness or darkness of a color (imagine where it would fall on a grayscale from white to black).

Contrast in Saturation and Intensity
Saturation refers to the purity of a hue. Pure, saturated colors are bright. They can be modified by adding white (tints) or black (shades). A color's intensity can be changed by adding portions of its complement (when mixed, complementary colors form neutrals or brown). A great deal of contrast can be gained by pairing a bright color with a neutral.

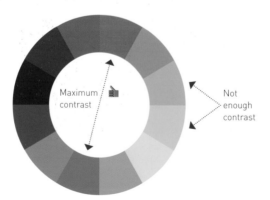

←

Distance between segments on the color wheel is an indicator of hue contrast. Colors positioned close together are more difficult to differentiate. Complementary colors— those in opposite positions on the wheel—have maximum hue contrast. However, value contrast should also be a consideration. Complementary colors that have the same value can create simultaneous contrast, which frequently causes eye strain.

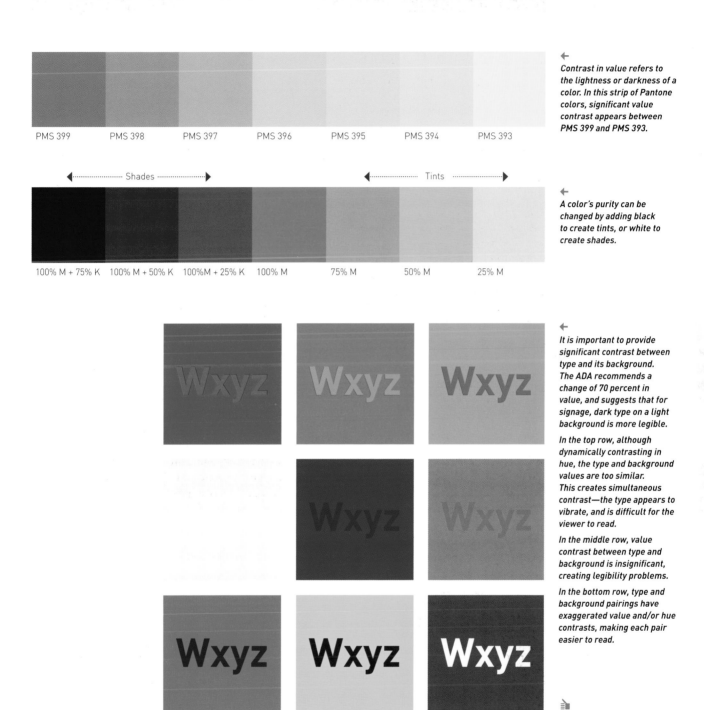

| PMS 399 | PMS 398 | PMS 397 | PMS 396 | PMS 395 | PMS 394 | PMS 393 |

←

Contrast in value refers to the lightness or darkness of a color. In this strip of Pantone colors, significant value contrast appears between PMS 399 and PMS 393.

◀·········· Shades ··········▶   ◀·········· Tints ··········▶

| 100% M + 75% K | 100% M + 50% K | 100%M + 25% K | 100% M | 75% M | 50% M | 25% M |

←

A color's purity can be changed by adding black to create tints, or white to create shades.

←

It is important to provide significant contrast between type and its background. The ADA recommends a change of 70 percent in value, and suggests that for signage, dark type on a light background is more legible.

In the top row, although dynamically contrasting in hue, the type and background values are too similar. This creates simultaneous contrast—the type appears to vibrate, and is difficult for the viewer to read.

In the middle row, value contrast between type and background is insignificant, creating legibility problems.

In the bottom row, type and background pairings have exaggerated value and/or hue contrasts, making each pair easier to read.

117

Orientation

An object's orientation (right-side up, upside down, sideways, diagonal), relative to other elements in the composition, can create meaning by focusing attention on anomaly. Orientation can also be linked with motion.

Position

Position refers to the physical location of an object within a frame of reference. Dramatic or unexpected shifts in position can create dynamic contrast, or change visual focus. Alignment of position implies connectivity. Position, like orientation, is often linked with motion.

Shape

We often ascribe personality, meaning, or emotion to different shapes (as we do with colors). Circles are more "fun" than squares because they remind us of things that bounce. Curvilinear, organic shapes are more natural, sensual, and creative than those that are geometric. And geometric shapes may allude to precision, math, or science. Contrasts of shape therefore engage both our ability to notice form, and our cognitive associations with those configurations.

Size

Size has an immediate correlation with worth or significance. The size of one object compared to another can influence context, hierarchy, and meaning.

Texture

Shifts in tactile quality or pattern can create focal points, or differentiate information sets.

Weight

The optical weight of an object is a visual cue to its hierarchical importance. By altering this attribute, designers can make objects dominant or recessive. For example, line elements of various weights can be used to guide a viewer through successive steps in a set of instructions. A bold line might separate each step, with lighter lines used to subdivide information within those sections.

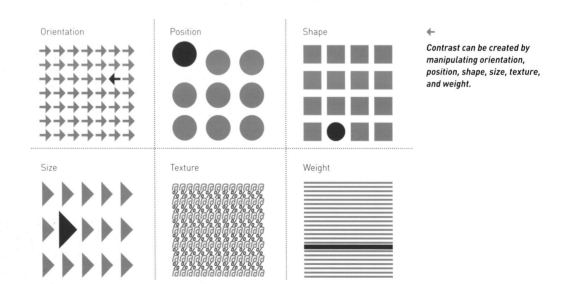

← *Contrast can be created by manipulating orientation, position, shape, size, texture, and weight.*

For more information on how contrast works from a
cognitive perspective, read these theories in Chapter 4:
  · **The Gestalt Principles of Perception (p. 64)**
  · **Difference Threshold (p. 62)**
  · **Eye Tracking (p. 66)**

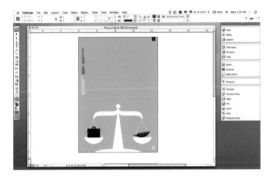

↑
**When working, periodically
change your monitor to
grayscale to check the value
contrast of your work. In the
Mac OS X operating system,
this option is located in
System Preferences under
Universal Access.**

Quick Tips

Go grayscale
When designing in color, do a quick check
of value contrast by turning your monitor
to grayscale or printing to a grayscale
printer. If graphic elements and typography
appear to blend together, adjust the colors
accordingly to create more contrast.

Less and more
You don't need to incorporate every form of
visual contrast to create a dynamic layout.
Instead, pick a single contrast pair and
really maximize the concept (for example,
turn big/small into huge/tiny).

Provide stability
Is contrast dependent on continuity?
In complex information sets, yes. The
hierarchical effects created by contrast
lose their value if there's no place for
the viewer's eye to rest. So use familiar
structures and type treatments to support
dramatic effect.

Legibility

Typography

All of the aesthetic principles in this chapter can apply to typography. However, type has unique characteristics, and specific issues must be borne in mind when making typographic decisions for information design projects.

Attentiveness to legibility and readability will help the end user access your message clearly. While to the layperson these two words may sound like synonyms, typographically speaking they are quite different.

Legibility refers to the traits that affect recognition of individual letters and words. As we read, we recognize the shape of familiar words, rather than processing each single letter to make a phonetic group. This allows us to process content much faster. The legibility of type can be discussed in terms of shape, scale, and style.

Readability refers to clarity and the speed at which typographic content can be read in large quantities (paragraphs, pages, volumes). Readability is related to a font's legibility but is also subject to design and layout decisions. Assuming that the type is legible, readability is a function of size, spacing, and alignment.

A typeface with high legibility/readability can be read much more quickly than one with low legibility/readability. That classification alone doesn't render the typeface good or bad, but rather indicates its suitability for specific tasks. While a script font might set the appropriate tone for your cousin's wedding invitations, imagine trying to navigate with street signs set the same way. That's why fonts are often classified as "display" or "text." Think of the former as appropriate in small doses, while the latter are suitable for more intensive reading. You might also consider how quickly your user needs to access the information you're delivering (there's a reason why Exit signs aren't set in Soda Script). On every project, designers make choices that balance stylistic needs with direct communication issues. Close attention to legibility and readability can help inform those choices.

People read the shapes of whole words, not the individual letters themselves

← *Readers recognize the shapes of familiar words, rather than reading each individual letter.*

Typographic Legibility Considerations

Shape

In typography, shape is discussed in terms of form and counterform. Form refers to the positive shapes, or straight and curved lines (strokes) that make a letter. Counterforms (sometimes simply referred to as counters) are the negative spaces knocked out of the letterform—the half-circles forming a lowercase "e," for example. The relationship between the positive stroke and the negative counter affects the legibility, or quick recognition, of the letter. Too much contrast, on either side of the equation, makes it difficult to read quickly. If a font has extremely thick strokes with very small counters it takes longer for the eye to decode it as an alphabetical shape. Conversely, if a font has extremely thin strokes with very large counters it requires more visual effort to decipher the form from the negative space. The most legible fonts have a well-balanced proportion of form and counterform.

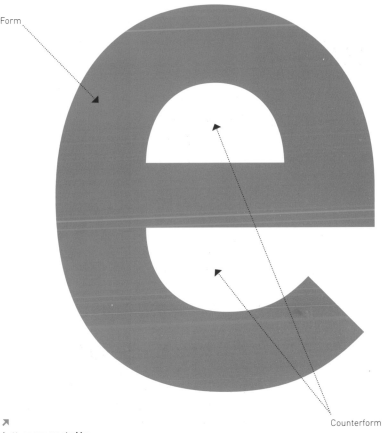

Form

Counterform

↗
Letters are created by positive and negative shapes. The positive shape is referred to as the form, the negative shape is called the counterform, or counter.

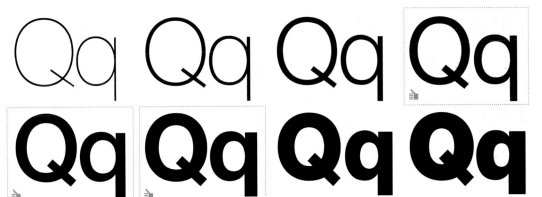

←
The ratio of form to counterform plays an important role in a letter's legibility. When strokes are very thin, and counters large, the letter is more difficult to identify, and similarly with thick strokes and small counters. Letters exhibiting a well-balanced proportion of form and counterform are the most legible.

Scale

The scale of a letterform is dictated by a number of proportional factors, including:

X-height to Cap Height: The term "x-height" describes the height of the main body of lowercase letters in a given typeface—not including the ascenders (the upward strokes on b, d, f, h, k, l, t) and descenders (the downward strokes on g, j, p, q, y). It is measured by the height of the lower case "x," hence the name. "Cap height" is the measurement of the capital letters from the baseline (an imaginary line upon which the letters sit) to the top. Each typeface has a unique ratio between the height of its capital and lowercase letters, which is instrumental in its overall legibility. Typefaces exhibiting tall x-heights are thought to be easier to read because they appear larger than those exhibiting short x-heights when viewed at the same point size. But exaggerated x-heights at either extreme negatively affect legibility as they distort the commonly recognized shape of the letterform.

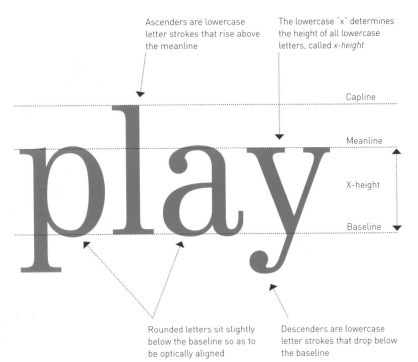

The length of ascenders and descenders, in relation to the main body of the letter, can affect legibility. Short ascenders make letters such as "d" and "b" difficult to differentiate. Typographers work to balance x-height with the lengths of ascenders and descenders.

Ascenders are lowercase letter strokes that rise above the meanline

The lowercase "x" determines the height of all lowercase letters, called *x-height*

Capline

Meanline

X-height

Baseline

Rounded letters sit slightly below the baseline so as to be optically aligned

Descenders are lowercase letter strokes that drop below the baseline

The x-height of a typeface plays a key role in its legibility. For example, this is 15pt Baskerville.

This is 15pt Helvetica Neue 55. Looks bigger, doesn't it? That's because it has a taller x-height.

15pt Mrs. Eaves! Now that is a small x-height!

X-height is determined by the height of the lowercase "x" in a typeface. Higher x-heights appear more legible, especially at smaller sizes.

Width to Height: A font's width-to-height ratio determines how wide each letter appears. The most legible typefaces have fairly equal width-to-height ratios. Imagine that each letter loosely forms a square. When that balance tips and the width is significantly greater than the height, the typeface becomes "Extended." Imagine a letter in that scenario forming a horizontal rectangle. When the balance tips significantly in favor of height, the font is called "Condensed." Imagine those letters as vertical rectangles. Letters that are too wide or too narrow decrease legibility.

Stroke Width to Height: The relationship between stroke width and height determines the optical weight of the letterform, making it light, regular, bold, etc. Increases or decreases in stroke weight have a direct effect on the form and counterform of the letter—which, as discussed previously, affects legibility. Extremely thin and extremely heavy fonts are harder to read than those of average width (often called Regular).

↗
A letter's width-to-height ratio is another important factor in legibility. Letters that appear very tall and thin, or wide and fat, negatively affect rapid recognition. For both legibility and readability purposes, a balanced proportion is best.

→
Form and counterform are affected by changes in stroke weight. Thin fonts exaggerate counterform, and heavy fonts exaggerate form. Both extremes make the letters harder to recognize and read quickly.

Type
Univers 39 Thin Ultra Condensed

Type
Univers 65 Bold

Type
Univers 93 Extra Black Extended

Type
Univers 45 Light

Type
Univers 65 Bold

Type
Univers 85 Extra Black

Style

Type comes in numerous styles: serif and sans serif, display and text, roman and italic, classic and experimental, to name only a few. Different styles can evoke emotional responses. Editorially, a font may appear whimsical, serious, edgy, romantic, clinical— the possibilities are endless. While there may be an appropriate application for just about every typeface under the sun, not all are suitable for the purposes of information design. When delivering a clear, unambiguous message directly to a specific audience, type choices should focus on accessibility. The most versatile typefaces are balanced in weight and proportion, and should possess no anomalous forms, decorative details, or exaggerated characters. Whether serif or sans, historically crafted or created with Fontographer, successful information design type selections have distinct individual letterforms that are easily recognized on their own and feel unified when in a group.

ROSEWOOD

Brush Script

FILOSOFIA

Display

Helvetica

Centennial

Verdana

Text

↑

Most typefaces can be divided into one of two categories: display fonts, which are decorative; and text fonts, designed for readability and versatility. When choosing fonts, think carefully about which category is appropriate for the intended use. (Imagine

trying to read a novel set in Rosewood, or being excited about a circus advertised in Helvetica.)

The three fonts at the top represent display choices.

The three fonts below represent text choices.

Helvetica and Centennial were designed specifically for print purposes, Verdana specifically for the web.

Typographic Readability Considerations

Size

We've all experienced the correlation between type size and readability, whether we're squinting to read the fine print in a contract, struggling through large quantities of text on the web, or missing a turning due to a poorly sized street sign. There are a number of dimensional adjustments that can make written content easier for the user to access.

Type Size

Type size is measured differently according to medium. In print design, type is measured in points (there are 72 points in an inch, or 28.35 points in a centimeter). Web design measures type in ems—an em is an international standard of measurement in which one unit is equal to the point size of the font currently in use. Ems are a dynamic measurement, so when a user sets his or her on-screen size preferences, the type scales proportionally—merging the designer's aesthetic vision directly with the user's viewing needs. Environmental design references type size in terms of architectural measurements (Imperial Units, US Customary Units, or the Metric System).

Choosing the correct type size is driven by variables of font design, application, and audience. When designing for the elderly or visually impaired, special provision should be made.[1] Proven rules about type size are hard to find and debate continues to rage among typographers. The following axioms, combined with a strong understanding of the user's needs and a little bit of common sense, should guide you in the right direction:

In the book Stop Stealing Sheep & Find Out How Type Works, expert typographer Erik Spiekermann (designer of the Meta and Officina type families) suggests that printed body copy should be no smaller than 9 points and no larger than 14. These measurements apply to traditional type styles and x-height plays a crucial role in making size determinations.

The low resolution of computer monitors, combined with the general distance between our eyes and the screen, create different size requirements for typographic content online. Several usability studies[2] have indicated that setting online body copy at a size equivalent to 12–14 points increases the time a user will spend reading a web page. Remember the equation: 12 points = 16 pixels = 1 em (approximately).

When determining type size for environmental signage or exhibit design, always consider the distance between the viewer and the content. Additional environmental factors such as lighting and atmosphere may determine a need for increased dimensions (see p. 126).

1. For more information about designing for the aging eye, see "Typography and Older Viewers" on p. 111.

2. For more about desired line lengths for web design, read Usability News (a software usability research newsletter from Wichita State University) vol. 4, issue 2, "The Effects of Line Length on Children and Adults' Online Reading Performance" and vol. 7, issue 2, "The Effects of Line Length on Reading Online News."

Baskerville 9pt	Futura 9pt
Baskerville 12pt	Futura 12pt
Bodoni 9pt	Helvetica 9pt
Bodoni 12pt	Helvetica 12pt
Garamond 9pt	Univers 9pt
Garamond 12pt	Univers 12pt

←

Text copy sizes ideally range between 9 and 12 points. Here are some popular serif and sans-serif options shown at those sizes. Note the optical differences due to changes in x-height.

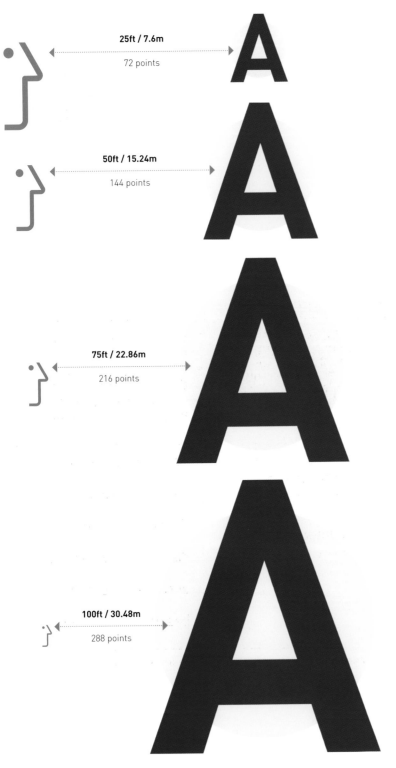

25ft / 7.6m
72 points

50ft / 15.24m
144 points

75ft / 22.86m
216 points

100ft / 30.48m
288 points

Column Width and Line Length

Line lengths and column widths have a direct impact on our ability to access information rapidly. If columns are too narrow, words become hyphenated and viewers are unable to grab a significant amount of content in their scan path. If columns are too wide, our eyes have difficulty relocating the starting point of each new line of text. Both can create eye strain and adversely affect reading time.

Over the last century, several scientific studies have been conducted to determine the readability of different line lengths. Early studies of print found that line lengths of approximately 4in (10cm) were the most readable. Contemporary studies of online text suggest 7in (18cm) line lengths to be optimal for that medium.[4]

→
Narrow columns can create an awkward reading experience by creating truncated lines of type. Conversely, columns that are too wide can make reading difficult because the reader may have a difficult time locating the starting point of the next line of text.

←
When designing typography for an environmental application, the ADA suggests an increase of 72 points for every 25 feet / 7.6 meters of viewing distance.

Line lengths and column widths have a direct impact on our ability to access information rapidly. If columns are too narrow, words become hyphenated and the viewer is unable to grab a significant amount of information.

Spacing

Spatial considerations, from minute adjustments between letter pairs to the density of entire paragraphs, can affect the ease and speed with which we process text. Typographic intervals are discussed in terms of leading and letter spacing:

Leading

Leading, sometimes called line spacing, defines the vertical distance between lines of type (measured from baseline to baseline). It is another factor that affects the readability of typography. Leading variations within a design create a tonal palette for text and can enhance hierarchy decisions. However, in terms of long-term readability, moderate line spacing is optimal. When leading is too tight it can interrupt the natural flow of reading, creating areas of tension caused by colliding ascenders and descenders. Tight leading can also detract from our ability to recognize individual words by camouflaging their shapes with awkward negative spaces. Conversely, when leading is too loose, it can slow reading time and hinder our ability to locate the starting point of the next line of type in a paragraph of text. Most page-layout applications set the default leading to 120 percent of the type point size for maximum readability (for example, 10pt type would sit on 12pt leading).

→

Leading, the spacing between lines of type, can affect the readability of typography. When the leading is too tight, ascenders and descenders collide, rendering text illegible. When the leading is too loose, it is difficult for the viewer to locate the start of the next line of text, particularly if combined with a long line length.

4. For a more detailed overview of studies on optimal line length, read "Optimal Line Length" from the *UI Design Newsletter*, November 2002. Available at http://www.humanfactors.com/downloads/nov02.asp

Negative Leading: 12/10

Leading, sometimes called line spacing, defines the vertical distance between lines of type (measured from baseline to baseline).

Set Solid: 12/12

Leading, sometimes called line spacing, defines the vertical distance between lines of type (measured from baseline to baseline).

Leading, sometimes called line spacing, defines the vertical distance between lines of type (measured from baseline to baseline).

Leading, sometimes called line spacing, defines the vertical distance between lines of type (measured from baseline to baseline).

Approximately 120%: 12/14

Approximately 200%: 12/24

Letter spacing

Letter spacing is the act of adjusting the horizontal space between letters.

Kerning describes adjustments to the space between two individual letters. Improper kerning can create areas of visual tension or strange gaps between letter pairs that can impair reading.

Tracking is the adjustment of space in a word, line, or paragraph of text. When tracking is too tight, letters lose their individual character, bumping or optically blending together and making words more difficult to distinguish. If tracking is too loose, the letters appear to be floating and words are equally difficult to discern. Remember, theories suggest that we read words by recognizing their shape instead of phonetically composing the individual letters, so distorting those shapes will affect readability.

↗
Though the computer has revolutionized the speed at which designers work, especially in regard to typesetting, there are still a few things that software doesn't do as well as humans. Kerning is one of them. The word above, set automatically by page-layout software, features a few kerning pairs that seem just a little too far apart. Individual adjustments to spacing (shown in the word below) create a more cohesive reading experience. Be especially sensitive to kerning issues when setting headlines or signage.

→
Tracking adjusts the spacing between multiple letters, from a single word to an entire paragraph. Tracking changes can affect readability. When letters are too tightly spaced, the shape of the word is difficult to recognize; the same is true if the letters are too loose. When tracking uppercase letters for signage purposes, the ADA suggests 110 percent as the optimal amount for legibility.

Kerning
Kerning

Tracking
-100 Optical Tracking

Tracking
Normal Optical Tracking

Tracking
+100 Optical Tracking

Alignment

Paragraphs or groupings of type can be aligned in several different ways. The axis point can be central, left, or right. Text can also be set so that both sides of the column are aligned, or justified. The unaligned side of the paragraph that creates a more jagged shape is called the "rag." In Western cultures, because we read from top to bottom, left to right, left-aligned type is the easiest for the viewer to read rapidly. The straight left axis creates a common starting point for the eye to quickly scan each line of text. When large quantities of copy are aligned to the right or center, the inconsistency of the rag edge makes it more difficult for the reader to find the starting point from line to line. Thus the same audience would process this information much more slowly, and probably with eye fatigue. Justified text also provides that straight left line that Western readers crave. But because both sides of the column are aligned, the spacing of the text within becomes inconsistent, causing noticeable white spots to appear between words. This phenomenon is referred to as "rivers of white," and these negatively affect readability by distracting the viewer from the continuity of the text.

→

Text alignment can affect readability, especially when reading large quantities. Flush-left text is easiest to read for long periods, as the axis provides an easily located starting point for each line, and the "rivers of white" (spots of negative space between words) found in justified text are eliminated.

Flush Left / Rag Right

Paragraphs or groupings of type can be aligned in several different ways. The axis point can be central, left, or right. Text can also be set so that both sides of the column are aligned, or justified. The unaligned side of the paragraph that creates a more jagged shape is called the "rag."

Center Axis

Paragraphs or groupings of type can be aligned in several different ways. The axis point can be central, left, or right. Text can also be set so that both sides of the column are aligned, or justified. The unaligned side of the paragraph that creates a more jagged shape is called the "rag."

Flush Right / Rag Left

Paragraphs or groupings of type can be aligned in several different ways. The axis point can be central, left, or right. Text can also be set so that both sides of the column are aligned, or justified. The unaligned side of the paragraph that creates a more jagged shape is called the "rag."

Justified

Paragraphs or groupings of type can be aligned in several different ways. The axis point can be central, left, or right. Text can also be set so that both sides of the column are aligned, or justified. The unaligned side of the paragraph that creates a more jagged shape is called the "rag."

Futura

Univers

← Choose typefaces that complement each other. Pair a serif with a sans serif for clear shape contrast to differentiate the fonts.

Futura
Clarendon

Bodoni

Clarendon

Quick Tips

Type suggestions from the ADA

According to ADA guidelines for accessible signage, characters on signs should possess a width-to-height ratio between 3:5 and 1:1.

ADA guidelines also suggest that point size (cap height) should increase by 1in (2.54cm, or 72 points) for every 25ft (7.62m) of distance.

Create the perfect match

Pairing a serif font with a sans-serif font creates clear typographic contrast. Avoid pairing two different sans serifs, or two different serifs, as the average reader doesn't immediately observe the difference (thus confusing the hierarchy).

Don't yell at the reader

Setting type in capital letters certainly makes a word or a line stand out. However, setting whole paragraphs that way negatively affects readability (and possibly tone).

Make accessible type choices

Serif fonts with extreme thick/thin stroke contrast, such as Bodoni, may be beautiful but can be difficult for some viewers to process because hairline strokes may blur or disappear, especially at small text sizes.

Learn the two-step

To enhance hierarchy, try using two steps of differentiation in your type choices. For example, if body copy is text-sized and black, make captions smaller and italic, or subheads larger and a different color. Apply the two-step technique to your entire type system.

For more information on how cognition affects typography, read these theories in Chapter 4:
- *The Gestalt Principles of Perception (p. 64)*
- *Difference Threshold (p. 62)*

For more information on how typographic principles connect with communication paradigms, read these theories in Chapter 5:
- *LATCH (Location, Alphabet, Time, Category, Hierarchy) Organization (p. 82)*
- *The Principle of Least Effort (p. 86)*
- *Uncertainty Reduction Theory (p. 88)*

Case Studies:
Locate, Perform, Understand

Information design is a vast subject, practiced by numerous disciplines and producing an enormous quantity of diverse artifacts. What unites the field is a focus on the end user, and the purposeful intent of each project. Information design can help the user perform tasks of varying complexity, from stopping at a railroad crossing to pitching a tent or recording a song. It can assist in location, indicating place and orientation in both physical and virtual environments—perhaps even political, social, or economic climates. As a rule, information design provides understanding.

This section provides a broad overview of international case studies designed to inform, and selected to inspire. With the focus always on the intended audience, the following examples are organized by user actions: Locate, Perform, and Understand. For a deeper insight into this critical design practice, learn from the experts and the experiments that are defining this extensive field.

Featuring Case Studies From:

Adams + Associates Design Consultants, Inc.

**Justice Mapping Center (JMC) &
Spatial Information Design Lab (SIDL)
at Columbia University**

Kick Design, Inc.

**Los Angeles County Metropolitan
Transportation Authority (Metro)**

Pentagram Design

Sussman/Prejza & Co., Inc.

Case Study

TBG Signage
and Wayfinding

Company

Adams + Associates
Design
Consultants, Inc.

Design Team

Design
Debbie Adams,
RGD

Technical Drawings
Sonia Gulia

*Industrial Design
Consultation*
David Dennis

Client

Toronto Botanical
Garden (TBG)

Audience

TBG members
and patrons,
gardening and
horticulture
enthusiasts,
tourists

Fertile Ground

The splendor of nature is a tough act to compete with, so designer Debbie Adams decided to collaborate instead.

Adams, one of Ontario's prestigious Registered Graphic Designers, was hired to create a new signage and wayfinding system for the Toronto Botanical Garden. Having just completed a major renovation, the institution was eager to produce exhibits that would engage visitors with their new space and make them enthusiastic about gardening.

Adams's commission would be a major influence on the visitor experience at the gardens—from wayfinding systems that designate amenities and make the space easy to navigate, to informational panels and kiosks that enrich the natural displays. Her work required integration with the garden's architecture, landscape design, and brand identity.

Abundant Variety

The wayfinding program is comprehensive, guiding visitors clearly through 4 acres and 12 themed gardens without detracting from their connection with nature. Directional indicators are thoughtfully positioned with attention to common sight lines, and material choices immediately differentiate them from the lush natural surroundings and informational displays.

Informational garden panels educate visitors about the plant life. These graceful structures are made out of metal and glass yet appear to arch effortlessly from the ground, mimicking the surroundings but with distinct geometric forms providing an element of contrast. Typographic systems are clean and elegant, clearly delineating a hierarchy of information. They are enhanced by detailed botanical illustrations. The design team also provided some interchangeable message areas, allowing TBG employees to update and change the content as appropriate for the seasons or specific events.

A donor recognition wall is comprised of eight subdivided panels, catching the visitor's eye with yet another dynamic combination of color, materials, and natural imagery. Major contributors are honored with a flourish of unfolding ferns, photographed with extreme detail and enlarged to dramatic proportions. Their organic verticals are complemented by the geometry of the panels, drawing the eye to the information sets above.

Reaping the Benefits of Good Design

Adams + Associates created a design system that enhances rather than competes with its environment. The carefully crafted aesthetic mimics the lithe shapes found in botany; it educates viewers and allows visitors to find their way easily through the space. The combined effect, when paired with the natural abundance of the gardens, leaves TBG visitors inspired to create their own green spaces—the essence of the organization's mission. And with accolades for the design's practicality, the team should be recognized for succeeding within an extremely tight budget, keeping the charitable organization "in the green."

The effectiveness of the finished design is evidenced by client satisfaction and industry recognition. The project was honored by both the Society for Environmental Graphic Design (SEGD) and the Registered Graphic Designers of Ontario.

→
The donor recognition wall artfully combines color, form, and image to catch the visitor's attention. The directional elements in the design lead the viewer's eye to contributor information.

entry garden walk and arrival courtyard

The Entry Garden Walk leads to the Arrival Courtyard. Dutch garden designer Piet Oudolf's New Wave style is introduced to Canadians who appreciate the challenge of creating all-season interest. Perennials, grasses, shrubs and trees were carefully selected for their architectural form, texture, autumn colour and winter silhouette. Planting is done in naturalistic waves that form a "sophisticated meadow". The plants were chosen for hardiness and sustainability. Tough specimens reward visitors with a garden that may look a little wild but is tame at heart.

The Arrival Courtyard, which lies at the end of the walk and forms the entry point to The George and Kathy Dembroski Centre for Horticulture, is a natural place to congregate. Plenty of seating surrounds the unique "living sculptures".

ENTRY GARDEN WALK

Donated by
The Garden Club of Toronto, 2006

←↖↑
The wayfinding and signage system developed by Adams + Associates Design Consultants for the Toronto Botanical Gardens is distinctive without diverting attention from the exhibits. Constructed out of aluminum, stainless steel, and glass, the materials evoke gardening supplies and are durable enough to stand up to fluctuations in temperature and humid or wet conditions.

Case Study

Million Dollar
Blocks Maps

Company

Justice Mapping
Center (JMC) &
Spatial Information
Design Lab (SIDL) at
Columbia University

Design Team

Eric Cadora (JMC),
Laura Kurgan
(SIDL), Charles
Swartz (JMC)

Client

Self-directed
project

Audience

Legislative officials,
policy makers, and
the general public

An Expensive Proposition

In the United States, more than two million Americans are behind bars, and the population is increasing every year.

New evidence shows that a disproportionate number of inmates come from the poorest neighborhoods in the largest cities. Sending people to jail is expensive. In the US, keeping one inmate in prison for a single year costs more than $30,000. The financial burden is carried by the taxpayer. At the end of their sentence, 95 percent of inmates return to their original home, and a staggering 40 percent of those released will end up back in jail. To better understand the geographic, social, political, and economic ramifications of this growing problem, Eric Cadora and Charles Swartz, cofounders of the Justice Mapping Center (JMC), teamed up with Laura Kurgan, a professor at Columbia University and director of the Spatial Information Design Lab (SIDL), to trace the migration patterns of prisoners.

The partnership gathered data from prison entry forms, using specialized mapping software to visualize the results. They began their study by dividing New York City into census blocks. They counted the number of people calling those blocks home who were currently incarcerated, multiplied each individual's minimum sentence by the yearly cost of incarceration, and then tallied total expenditures per block. This process uncovered several "Million Dollar Blocks," located in some of the poorest neighborhoods of the city, where entry, exit, and reentry in the prison system had become a revolving door.

The resulting maps represent criminal population density with color. Bright red indicates an area with a large proportion of its population in the prison system, and black areas represent neighborhoods not greatly affected by crime. Consider the Brownsville neighborhood of Brooklyn as an example. The 17-block area is blanketed by shades of red. In 2003, 109 of its citizens were jailed, resulting in $17 million of taxpayer expense. It is no coincidence that over 40 percent of Brownsville's residents live below the poverty level.

The SIDL clearly frames the study's impact: "The maps suggest that the criminal justice system has become the predominant government institution in these communities and that public investment in this system has resulted in significant costs to other elements of our civic infrastructure—education, housing, health, and family. Prisons and jails form the distant exostructure of many American cities today."

→

Data for the Million Dollar Blocks project was gathered from prison records and mapped with software used by law enforcement. The design team discovered a correlation between poverty and incarceration, bringing funding models for criminal rehabilitation into question.

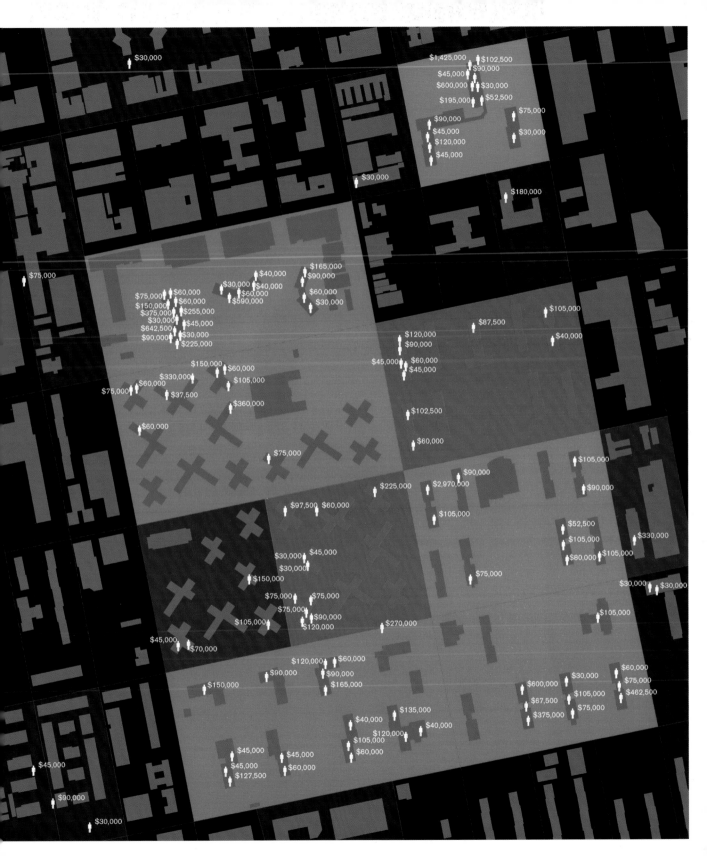

Challenging Conventional Thinking

The Million Dollar Blocks project succeeds by taking abstract data and weaving it into a story that is as straightforward as it is disturbing. The maps paint a somber picture of life in the neighborhoods awash with red. It is the hope of the team that their research will influence the ways in which legislative officials, policy makers, and the general public think about government spending—potentially redirecting some prison funding to invest instead in the communities that generate the most incarcerations. They have transformed their maps into multiple formats, seeking a broad audience. The results have even been displayed at MoMA. The project team has also partnered with the JFA Institute, a nonprofit organization that specializes in helping states implement new, more effective criminal justice policies and practices. As policy discussions evolve, the project team continues to incorporate input from state and local leaders in its spatial analysis. The ongoing study has grown to include examinations of Wichita, Kansas; Phoenix, Arizona; and New Orleans, Louisiana.

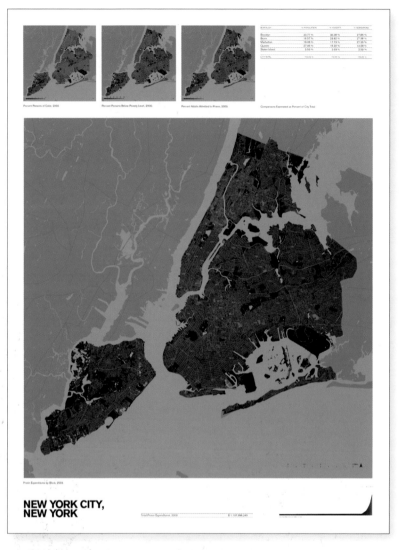

↗ →
What started out as an investigation of New York City census blocks has grown to include several other major metropolitan areas of the United States, including Wichita, Kansas; Phoenix, Arizona; and New Orleans, Louisiana.

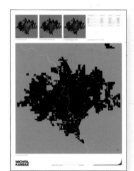
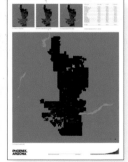
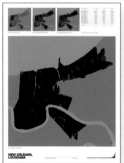

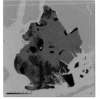

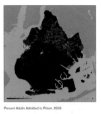

Percent Persons of Color, 2000.

Percent Persons Below Poverty Level, 2000.

Percent Adults Admitted to Prison, 2003.

COMMUNITY DISTRICT	% POPULATION	% POVERTY	% ADMISSIONS
CD 1	6.51 %	9.08 %	5.37 %
CD 2	4.03 %	3.58 %	4.64 %
CD 3	5.83 %	8.10 %	16.51 %
CD 4	4.24 %	6.34 %	9.34 %
CD 5	5.04 %	9.30 %	14.45 %
CD 6	4.23 %	2.60 %	3.08 %
CD 7	5.02 %	5.03 %	3.82 %
CD 8	3.78 %	4.15 %	9.46 %
CD 9	4.26 %	4.14 %	4.43 %
CD 10	4.96 %	2.79 %	0.91 %
CD 11	7.05 %	5.54 %	1.35 %
CD 12	7.99 %	8.54 %	1.32 %
CD 13	4.23 %	4.94 %	3.41 %
CD 14	6.76 %	6.22 %	3.79 %
CD 15	6.48 %	4.42 %	1.20 %
CD 16	3.48 %	5.92 %	8.43 %
CD 17	6.75 %	5.40 %	5.29 %
CD 18	7.96 %	3.91 %	3.20 %
BOROUGH TOTAL:	100.00 %	100.00 %	100.00 %

Comparisons Expressed as Percent of Borough Total.

Prison Expenditures by Block, 2003.

BROOKLYN, NEW YORK CITY

Total Prison Expenditures, 2003.	$ 359,988,750

ADDED UP BLOCK BY BLOCK, IT COST $359 MILLION DOLLARS TO IMPRISON PEOPLE FROM BROOKLYN EACH YEAR, FACILITATING A MASS MIGRATION TO PRISONS UPSTATE. 95% EVENTUALLY RETURN HOME.

← *The red lines on this map track the migratory patterns of inmates as they enter and exit the prison system. When their sentences expire, 95 percent return to their original home and a staggering 40 percent of those released end up back in jail.*

Case Study

Kickmap

Company

Kick Design, Inc.

Designer

Eddie Jabbour

Client

Self-directed project

Audience

NYC subway riders, local residents, visitors, and tourists

Organizing Spaghetti

Any visitor or recent arrival to New York City remembers their first glance at a subway map. It's overwhelming!

As one of the world's largest public transit systems, it's no surprise that there are dozens of routes and a myriad ways to reach your destination. Unfortunately, many users think that the current subway map, developed in 1979, reflects this complexity rather than clarifies it. Eddie Jabbour, Creative Director at Kick Design in NYC, saw the user experience through new eyes when he took a subway-dubious out-of-town client on a trek across the city. He's since devoted years of his personal time (perhaps with a hint of obsession) to finding a better solution.

Simplification as a Rule

Jabbour gathered hundreds of iterations of the New York subway map, analyzing them closely to determine best practices and avoidable mistakes. The resulting design, Kickmap, is the latest graphic incarnation of one of the world's most complex rail systems.

Kickmap places the needs of the user over geographic precision, stripping out extraneous information and focusing on passenger routes. The most radical shift from the current map is to remove the majority of non-subway transit lines, such as commuter railroads and buses. Kickmap is designed to address the subway system directly, and therefore only the most

commonly used connections need appear (bus lines that access airports, for example). Jabbour also introduces typographic changes, orienting word markers from left to right, consistent with Western reading patterns. By minimizing the flux of angled words and utilizing a common grid, Kickmap makes skimming and scanning easier for the average reader, enabling quick identification of train lines, transfers, and stations.

All rail lines on the Kickmap are representational, traveling straight or at stylized angles, instead of being literal reproductions of the train's path. This provides a clearer, grid-based structure and makes the map easier to navigate—particularly when most users are unaware of (or uninterested in) subtle shifts in direction that ultimately don't affect their route choice or end destination.

Kickmap illustrates each individual rail line, allowing the user to quickly differentiate local from express trains, or travel options based on time of day (many schedules change on evenings and weekends). In contrast, the current map uses one "trunk" to represent multiple subway lines sharing a track, which can make determining which train to ride a gamble.

An Ongoing Effort

Jabbour has met with the transit authorities, but NYC's Metropolitan Transportation Authority (MTA) has yet to adopt the new map. Remaining a champion for usability, Jabbour is still advocating the redesign and his effort has not gone unnoticed. Kickmap has been discussed in several magazines, websites, and newspapers—including *The New York Times*. In 2007, New York University held a gallery exhibit comparing Jabbour's new design to the existing 1979 map. He hopes that this type of exposure will heighten awareness and eventually result in the adoption of Kickmap. Until then, as a labor of love, the project continues with regular updates from ongoing research and feedback. Ultimately, Jabbour would like to see the map adopted by the MTA, but for now he's pleased that his mother, who lives in the Midwest, can easily find her way around when she comes to visit.

↖
Recognizing numerous usability problems with the official MTA New York City Subway map, local designer Eddie Jabbour decided to create a version that made navigating the city easy for residents and visitors alike.

→
Kickmap shows each train line to indicate the difference between local and express trains, transfer points, and schedules. Trains sharing common tracks also share color themes.

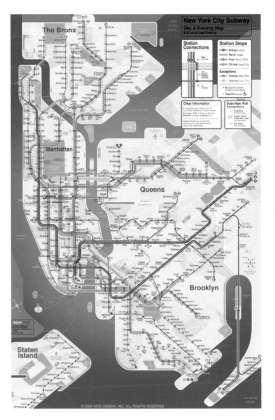

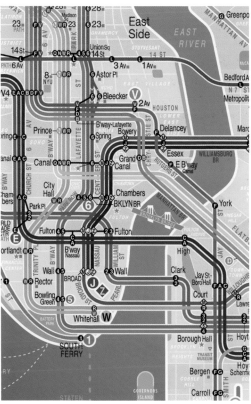

←
Kickmap focuses on the user, positioning type and image content on a clear grid structure. Stop names run horizontally, rather than matching the angle of the line. The subway routes run in straight paths or at stylized angles. Even landscape features are simplified. This departure from more traditional cartography allows for rapid determination of travel routes, eschewing unnecessary detail.

Case Study

Metro Orange
Line Project

Company

Los Angeles County
Metropolitan
Transportation
Authority (Metro)

Design Team

Metro Design
Studio

Client

In-house project

Audience

9.6 million local
residents
(nearly one-third of
the population of
California)

A New Direction

Southern Californians are famously addicted to their cars.

That leaves the Los Angeles County Metropolitan Transportation Authority (Metro) regularly challenged to inspire citizens to take advantage of mass transit. One promising solution to smog-filled skies and traffic jams clogged with commuters is the Orange Line, a rapid transit solution featuring dedicated roads used exclusively by Metro buses. Functionally similar to a train, but powered by unique 60ft (18m) buses called Metro Liners, the Orange Line is a new concept in So Cal public transportation. The advent of the line provided challenges for the in-house design team, too. Metro Design Studio, led by Creative Director Michael LeJeune, was tasked with creating a comprehensive campaign to introduce a new style of public transportation, generate riders, and help users successfully navigate new routes and buses.

Paving the Way

Prior to starting design work, the studio's creative team traveled the Orange Line to experience and visualize the route's landscape. "We studied the surrounding neighborhoods and businesses, armed with cameras to record details," says LeJeune. "The ethnographic experience guided us throughout the creative process. Design Studio members visited future stations while under construction to determine optimal signage solutions and grand opening banner placement. We even sat behind [noise attenuation] soundwalls to test the barriers firsthand, and rode our bikes on the bike path parallel to the route. It was definitely a hands-on research project."

Metro Design Studio used this research to craft accurate and consistent messaging throughout the Orange Line campaign. "Our philosophy was to keep everything simple yet functional; narrow information to only the most important details," says LeJeune. As part of the Metro system, the Orange Line also needed to adhere to graphic standards which integrate station signage and wayfinding concepts for all lines. Accessibility is key, as many riders are non-native English speakers, so pictographic symbols and markers are of special importance. The familiar Metro logo is positioned prominently throughout. The distinctive color selected to brand the Orange Line provides instant visual identification of related stations, buses, and marketing material. The bold color choice was also practical, heightening motorist awareness of traffic pattern changes at intersections.

Beyond quick-read aesthetics, Metro was sensitive to setting a tone for the line, directly addressing negative stereotypes about public transportation by creating a vision of a socially, environmentally, and economically responsible modern rider. Snappy copywriting and groovy imagery entice new audiences. Contemporary stainless steel design elements are found throughout the system, integrating with the buses themselves. Inclusion of public artwork transforms potentially drab shelters into exciting modern landmarks. Cycling paths are easily accessible, providing additional transportation, recreation, and fitness opportunities.

They're Lining Up

Metro's extensive research and attention to detail have generated measurable results. First-year ridership was triple the projections, and customer surveys and feedback from the press confirm community approval and commuter participation. In a region plagued by traffic jams, ozone alerts, and carbon emissions, the success of the Orange Line delivers much more than personal convenience and affordable transportation. A clear message has arrived.

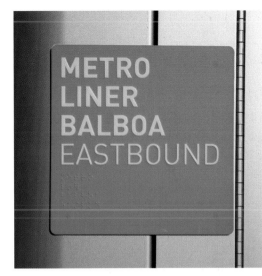

← ↑
The Orange Line builds on Metro's existing graphic standards while adding some punch of its own. Shown here: the distinctive color that visually brands the line; wayfinding signage; pictograms denoting a bicycle-friendly path.

←
A key component of the Orange Line's success is its integrated marketing campaign. Much more than a traditional wayfinding project, the designers at Metro utilized bright colors, compelling imagery, and great writing to build a buzz about a new style of public transportation.

↓

Case Study

Interactive Model of Lower Manhattan

Company

Pentagram Design

Design Team

Creative Director
Lisa Strausfeld

Designer and Programmer
Nina Boesch

Project Coordinator
Kate Wolf

Production Coordinator
Leslie Kang

Client

Wall Street Rising

Audience

Visitors, native New Yorkers, and tourists

Living History, Forecasting Opportunity

Scale models, used to describe a building's size, shape, and relationship to its environment, are a familiar tool in architecture. They provide three-dimensional context for a design.

But beyond issues of form and proximity, the communication potential of models is limited by their static nature. What would happen if a traditional scale model merged with video, audio, and interactive technology? Pentagram Design partner Lisa Strausfeld found the perfect opportunity to explore this question.

The firm had been hired by Wall Street Rising, a nonprofit organization dedicated to restoring the vibrancy and vitality that existed in Lower Manhattan prior to the devastating events of September 11, 2001. Seeking to draw patrons to their Downtown Information Center, Wall Street Rising engaged Pentagram to attract attention to their cause. Strausfeld's team envisioned an interactive experience that would help visitors locate practical information about the area's shops, restaurants, and businesses; learn about the rich history of the region; and engage in local events. To achieve this goal, they needed to provide a unique overview of the New York Financial District.

A Communal Table

Designed around the concept of a communal table, Pentagram created a circular, plexiglass-encased model of the district. Containing more than 250 buildings, the scale model is 9ft (2.7m) wide by 11ft (3.4m) long and is a commanding piece of work. It offers common ground for people to gather and discover the area. Visitors control content using a gyro-mouse, and can select site-specific or educational information. Included are eight short documentary films written by author James Sanders and narrated by journalist John Hockenberry. These movies are projected onto the table and take visitors on a trip through time, starting with Dutch New Amsterdam in the seventeenth century and ending in the modern Financial District.

To create a dynamic experience, the technology had to be transparent, connecting casual visitors with the display, Lower Manhattan, and each other. To function as intended, the model required sophisticated planning, from fabrication to digital technology and content management. Physically, the table splits into three sections, allowing the Downtown Information Center to reconfigure their space when needed. All of the graphics are cast onto the 3-D model by two ceiling projectors, and designed in Flash. Pentagram also built a proprietary system that allows Wall Street Rising employees to update content regularly. The net result is not only beautiful to look at, it inspires exploration of both Wall Street Rising's mission and Lower Manhattan itself.

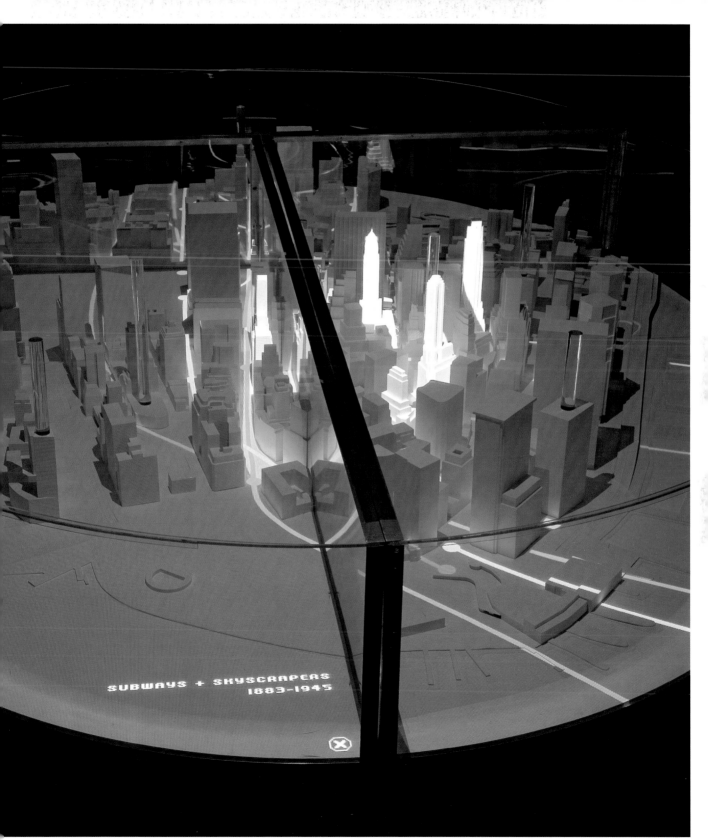

SUBWAYS + SKYSCRAPERS
1883-1945

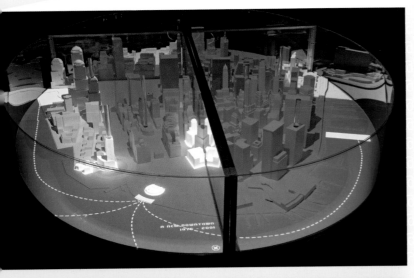

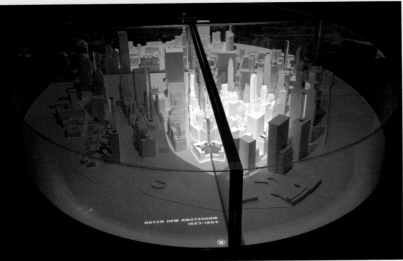

←↑
Visitors can activate different information sets, referencing historical or contemporary content. The model is shown here amid multiple animations, some featuring specific buildings, others entire blocks. Dramatic contrasts of lighting and color are projected onto the stark white model, clearly outlining the areas being discussed by the narrator.

→
Wall Street Rising's interactive model of Lower Manhattan explores the history, resources, and potential of the city's Financial District. Projected graphics activate the traditional architectural display.

Company

Sussman/Prejza
& Co., Inc.

Design Team

Deborah Sussman,
Paul Prejza, Randy
Walker, John
Johnston, Tad Hara,
Paul Nagakura,
Miles Mazzie, and
Hsin-Hsien Tsai

Client

Mori Building
Company

Audience

Residents, tourists,
and visitors

Creating a Community

Roppongi Hills is the largest privately funded integrated urban development in Tokyo, Japan. This city within a city contains upscale offices, entertainment, housing, and cultural attractions.

An inspiring place to work, play, and call home, the development was created to reduce commute times, improve efficiency, and provide residents—both commercial entities and individuals—with numerous intangible benefits.

In order to establish a unique sense of place, the Roppongi Hills development needed to differentiate itself clearly from the surrounding urban environment.

A wayfinding system evoking the neighborhood's brand and providing spatial direction for workers, residents, and visitors would become a crucial factor in achieving that goal. The American design firm Sussman/Prejza & Co. connected the Roppongi Hills identity to its physical environment, and in the process, defined a foundation for its lifestyle.

Collective Communication

Central to the design process, a great deal of preliminary research was undertaken to understand the place, its history, spirit, and unique characteristics. Roppongi Hills serves a diverse audience. For some it is home, for others a workplace, shopping district, cultural center, or vacation destination. The Sussman/Prejza design had to work for people who

would see it every day for many years, and for tourists who might only visit once in a lifetime. Signage needed to include identifications in both Japanese and English, making content accessible to visitors from around the world.

Continually referencing the Roppongi Hills brand identity, the Sussman/Prejza team created simple, easily identified environmental graphics. The core aesthetic references the circles occurring in the word "Roppongi." This circular emphasis is found throughout the campaign, from architectural elements to typography. Circular maps in outdoor kiosks provide survey knowledge for those new to the location. More abstract markers define boundaries, providing route-based information regarding the perimeter of the complex, while referencing a circular pattern based on the logotype. An impressive and imposing curved glass wall repeats the mark, etched into its enormous windowed surface. The results are both timeless and beautiful, and the aesthetic continuity clearly defines Roppongi Hills, requiring no effort on the part of its visitors—allowing them instead to marvel at one of Japan's most prestigious urban renewal projects.

Sussman/Prejza produced comprehensive wayfinding and environmental design for the prestigious Roppongi Hills development in Tokyo, Japan. They used graphic and architectural devices to visually separate the neighborhood from the surrounding urban area, while providing clear and accessible directions for a broad international audience.

Inspired by the letters in the word "Roppongi," Sussman/ Prejza incorporated circular elements throughout the campaign. Shown here are two maps from public kiosks in the development.

Featuring Case Studies From:

AdamsMorioka

Meeker & Associates and Terminal Design

Pentagram Design

Read Regular

Satellite Design

Scheme, LTD.

Studio Panepinto, LLC

Ultimate Symbol

Case Study

USC
Admissions
Marketing Plan

Company

AdamsMorioka

Design Team

Designer
Sean Adams

Research
Terry Stone
Noreen Morioka

Client

University of
Southern California
(USC) Office of
Admissions

Audience

Overall Campaign
Potential applicants
(especially target
groups of high-
school juniors and
seniors)

Marketing Plan
Internal Office of
Admissions staff

Kids These Days...

College kids have earned a reputation for being the most demanding consumers in history.

They make decisions based on dozens of constantly changing factors. They reject typical marketing tactics. So how do you figure out why a teenager chooses a particular college?

For Beverly Hills design firm AdamsMorioka, the obvious answer was lots of research—and the inspired use of those old information design standards, charts and grids.

The University of Southern California Office of Admissions wanted to investigate the broad demographic of the skeptical teen. AdamsMorioka began reviewing the challenges of the project immediately, and soon recognized the need for ongoing research and input from stakeholders throughout the life of the project. The resulting University of Southern California Marketing Plan (in its multiple drafts) provided a dynamic tool that facilitated detailed research and allowed AdamsMorioka to build the most effective design solutions for their client.

The Right Message

While most design projects begin after research concludes, AdamsMorioka chose a unique approach—their marketing plan encouraged the team to continue researching and honing the project up to the point of completion. Tasked with reaching specific groups of prospective students and their parents, AdamsMorioka had to build communications that demonstrated an understanding of how those respective groups approached college admissions during their final two years of high school.

Promoting Dialogue

The centerpieces for the marketing plan were 36 × 48in (91.4 x 121.9cm) charts that investigated the needs of a specific audience. Copies of these large boards were used by designers and and stakeholders alike, allowing each to add, alter, or remove ideas and information. This made AdamsMorioka extremely responsive to changing needs, data, and results during a project that spanned several years. The firm stayed in constant contact with its client and its audience, resulting in a remarkably effective campaign.

Identifying Needs

The large-format two-year-plan marketing charts considered the admissions process from the viewpoint of the audience—high-schoolers in their junior and senior years and their parents. Using a timeline approach and asking broad questions, the boards provoked discussion and helped the firm and their client think like the target audience. "We needed to show what the audience was doing, thinking, and feeling during the last two years of high school," says Sean Adams, partner with AdamsMorioka. Though their initial plan called for specific print and electronic pieces to launch at specific times, the charts helped illuminate additional opportunities. "This also showed the need for new materials, or alternative ways of speaking to the audience," adds Adams.

How it Worked

The charts were critical to project development. They were typically placed on a bulletin board, allowing different stakeholders to make multiple notations, fine-tune the plan, and build consensus. The initial document helped the client grasp the breadth of their communication needs, Adams says, while subsequent charts looked at the motivations and expectations of more specific groups of prospective students (high achievers, Hispanic, etc.). They helped the client identify needs and achieve goals. "As we discussed with the client initially, there is no grand unification theory," Adams continues. "One size and one plan will not fit all. Multiple approaches need to be applied to various audiences."

Hitting the Target

The AdamsMorioka plan helped to identify and pursue the students most likely to apply to USC. The firm used a combination of print and electronic communications that evolved weekly to take advantage of new data, allowing marketing pieces to speak to specific audiences based on their unique needs and circumstances. What started as a draft plan became a living document—one that helped forge a healthy and ongoing relationship between AdamsMorioka and USC. By consistently engaging with the client and audience, relentlessly researching, and clearly outlining needs, goals, and motivations, the firm built a communications program that has dramatically increased the number of admissions applications and acceptances, and the academic quality of accepted students.

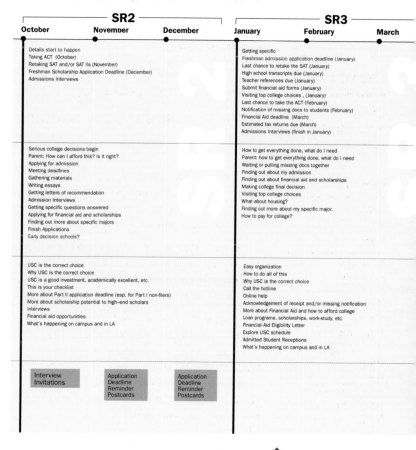

Chart detail.

→

AdamsMorioka used elaborate charts to build a marketing plan for the University of Southern California. Targeting high-school students in their junior and senior years, the design team collaborated with the Admissions department to collect and aggregate data that would determine the most appropriate vehicle and messaging for the campaign. This detailed process paid dividends, with applications, acceptances, and academic quality of accepted students all increasing.

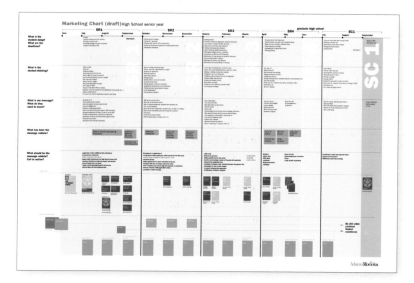

Company

Meeker &
Associates
and
Terminal Design

Design Team

Project leaders
Donald Meeker,
James Montalbano

Client

Self-directed
project

Audience

Motorists

An Unfocused Problem

Speeding down the road, looking for the nearest exit or rest stop, most people's thoughts are not focused on typography.

But perhaps they should be. Issues relating to sign legibility can mean both millions of dollars and scores of potential lives saved. Environmental graphic designer Donald Meeker and type designer James Montalbano decided to take on the ubiquitous highway sign, developing ClearviewHwy, a typeface designed specifically for modern roads and the needs of motorists.

Governmental transportation authorities have long recognized the problem of halation (the blurring of reflective signs at night, which disproportionately affects older drivers), but a uniform and effective solution was not readily apparent. One suggestion was to increase font size for better legibility, but this had many obstacles, including huge financial ramifications as the type-size change would necessitate larger signs. Meeker and Montalbano and their respective creative teams sought a typographic solution that focused on legibility and rapid word recognition, addressing the problems

of nighttime glare, as well as improving on existing fonts. Finding the answer would require considerable research and experimentation.

A Starting Point

The designers researched and compared numerous typefaces used for signs around the world, including Highway Gothic, found on most American road signs. They saw opportunities for improvement in all of them, but eventually decided to use Highway Gothic as a starting point. ClearviewHwy uses a taller x-height, larger counters, and increased letter spacing to accommodate the needs of older drivers and to reduce halation. Other features include some capital letters, such as B, D, P, and R, that break the cap line, as do the ascenders of lowercase b, d, f, h, i, j, k, and l. These details, among others, afford clear definition of letterforms and individual words, especially when viewed from a distance.

Field Work

Once a prototype was ready, testing of the typeface was extensive. The design team worked with researchers from the Pennsylvania Transportation Institute and 3M, manufacturer of reflective sign materials, to develop joint studies on the relationship between typeface design and halation. The designers performed legibility and recognition tests, paying particular attention to distances. In some scenarios, test subjects viewed actual

→
ClearviewHwy has been approved by the US Federal Highway Administration and is already in use in several states. This example was found on the roadway in Pennsylvania.

→
Words set in upper- and lowercase letters show an increase in accuracy, viewing distance, and reaction time when compared to those set entirely in uppercase. Put simply, we recognize the shape of the word before we're able to decipher each individual letter.

sign panels positioned on the Pennsylvania Transportation Institute test track, reading the signs from a moving car. In other experiments, subjects were asked to identify the position of a single word when set in groups of three, to test for recognition.

Successful Trip

With years of research and iteration, the designers were able to increase legibility by 16 percent. To put that in perspective, if a car is moving at 45mph (72km/h), ClearviewHwy affords the driver another 80ft (24m) of viewing distance, or approximately 1.2 seconds of additional reading time. This demonstrable improvement in recognition and dramatic reduction in halation occurs without resorting to larger font sizes or bigger signs.

So the next time someone tells you that type choices are purely artistic, you can tell them the story of ClearviewHwy—and likely point out an example from your car window, because the US Federal Highway Administration granted approval for use of the typeface on all US Federal roadways.

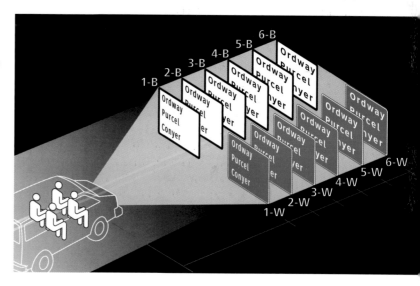

↑
ClearviewHwy has been visually optimized, and maintains greater word-pattern recognition for motorists with reduced contrast sensitivity. This example shows signs with an overglow or halation simulation.

↖
ClearviewHwy improves nighttime sign-reading distance by up to 16 percent. This illustration shows legibility distances for the various typefaces in the ClearviewHwy family.

Company

Pentagram Design

Design Team

Lead
Lisa Strausfeld

Design Team
Christian Marc
Schmidt,
Takaaki Okada

Client

One Laptop Per
Child Foundation

Audience

Children in
developing nations

Profound Change, One Laptop at a Time

Since their popular introduction in the 1980s, personal computers have become an integral part of our lives.

Long gone are the days of black screens, glowing green type, and multiple drive prompts. As users, we've benefited greatly from the development of graphical interfaces—so much so that even preschoolers are navigating digital landscapes. But consider how to introduce all the potential a computer represents to someone who has never used or even seen one. That was the challenge facing the team at Pentagram as they began to design a user interface for the XO, the computer created by the One Laptop Per Child (OLPC) Foundation to serve just such an audience.

OLPC is the culmination of massive creative, technical, and financial efforts. The organization's principal product, the XO, is a laptop computer designed to cost approximately $100 to produce. It was created to improve educational opportunities for more than two billion children in the developing world. Such a broad intended audience posed remarkable challenges for partner Lisa Strausfeld of Pentagram, as she designed the look and feel of Sugar, the XO's Linux-based operating system.

Because the children whose lives OLPC seeks to change are spread across the globe and are at varying educational levels, Sugar's user interface had to be profoundly intuitive, culturally and linguistically neutral, and highly adaptable. More importantly, the interface should inspire a child to want to actively engage with the machine, developing computer and information literacy skills that will serve them much longer than the laptop itself.

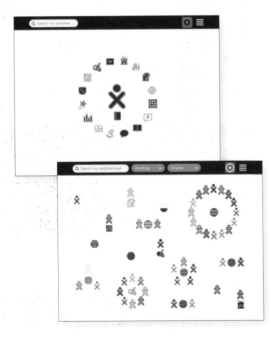

←←
Pentagram partnered with developers Red Hat and OLPC to create Sugar, the user interface for the XO laptop. Sugar focuses on activities rather than applications, using pictographic imagery to create a new, child-centered learning environment. Sugar is open source and OLPC has provided a developer wiki site to further its growth.

Shown here:

The top screenshot shows the user avatar surrounded by the available activities. The child can choose to play music, make art, connect with friends, and so on.

The second screenshot shows a Sugar neighborhood, where groups of users are playing, learning, and hanging out together. It's easy to see what kinds of activities are occurring, and then choose which to join.

Basic Machine, Basic Interface, Basic Opportunity

The XO is small, easy to use, approachable, durable, and inexpensive. Pentagram aimed to echo the hardware's attributes in the user interface. A small screen and other technical limitations confirmed the need for a simple graphic approach. Sugar's interface is a minimalist design built around activities, people, and objects, each represented by pictographic marks. The user avatar can be personalized, and children can organize their activities in different spheres: one might represent personal files and interests; another, things that are being shared, or a place where group activities occur.

Sugar's interface emphasizes community because of the proven pedagogical connection between sharing and learning. It's simple for users to connect because each laptop becomes a node on a mesh network, acting as its own wireless router, and distributing a signal that can be picked up by other local machines. The Sugar interface supports this connectivity by directly encouraging interaction among its users. They can "invite" or "join," showing each other how to surf the web by effortlessly sharing links, co-creating music or art, or collaboratively performing any number of educational tasks. In short, the user interface fosters a sense that each child is both a student and, potentially, a teacher.

Collaboration Abounds

The users aren't the only ones interacting. The Sugar interface is the product of teamwork, a triumph of research, imagination, design, and programming by visionaries at OLPC, Pentagram, and developers Red Hat. The very nature of OLPC's mission to spread the "light of learning" to the developing world ensures that this cooperation continues. And the results? They have the potential to change numerous lives for the better.

↓
OLPC (The One Laptop Per Child Foundation) has created the XO, which functions as a personal computer with open-source educational software and a uniquely targeted user interface—and as a wireless router. Each unit ultimately costs approximately $200 to produce and deliver to a child in a developing nation.

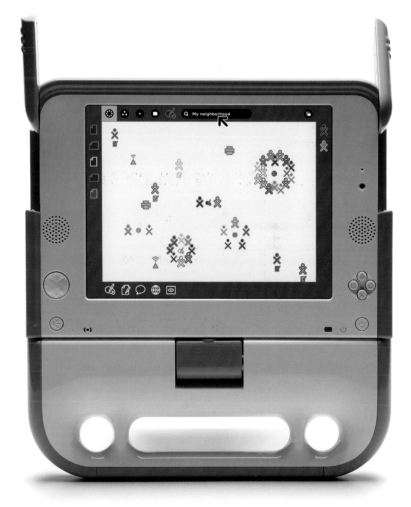

↓
Case Study

Read Regular
Type Design

Company

Read Regular

Designer

Natascha Frensch

Client

Self-directed
project

Audience

Readers with
dyslexia and
reading disorders,
and new readers

A New Approach

Awareness of the problems stemming from dyslexia and other reading disorders has been growing for decades, and new techniques for helping people overcome the associated challenges are constantly being developed and refined.

Many tactics—such as sight vocabulary, decoding skills, and word-recognition strategies—have helped millions of people overcome reading challenges to achieve their full potential. But amid the increased awareness and advances, designer Natascha Frensch noticed a fundamental element that had yet to be considered: the font.

Frensch set about designing a typeface with a completely new purpose. She developed Read Regular specifically to address the difficulties that accompany dyslexia. Each character in Read Regular has been formed to maximize differentiation between letters. For example, the stress and shape of the stroke and counter of the lowercase "b" are different from those of the lowercase "d" (instead of horizontally reflecting the same shape). Each letter that has mirrored shape relationships with another is treated in this way. This ensures that each character is distinctive and interfaces clearly with characters placed before and after it, thus boosting overall legibility. Frensch understood that this method could potentially produce an aesthetically disjointed alphabet, so she actively avoided superfluous details. The resulting typeface is simple and consistent, and, best of all, provides another level of clarity for its intended audience.

←
The use of Read Regular in the publishing industry is testament to its success. Shown here are several books using the typeface, from a series produced by Wayland, a publisher of children's educational books in the United Kingdom.

Experience, Research, and Sensitivity

While Read Regular was built to address issues for readers with dyslexia, anyone with reading difficulties can benefit from using the typeface, particularly new readers. Frensch considered the needs of young audiences and new readers from the start, drawing on her own childhood memories and experiences with the condition, and consulting with experts. Frensch actively researched dyslexia, reading disorders, and reading development at the start of the project. She also spent a great deal of time analyzing typography and type design. The resulting typeface greatly benefitted from the input of those working with dyslexia, teaching children, and from the opinions of other type designers.

Frensch mentions the need for subtle solutions, and she was cognizant of helping readers without drawing attention to their disabilities, stating: "Another primary goal I had was creating an inclusive typeface; one that is easy to read for all. For this, aesthetics are important. It should not look very different or stand out too much. Having difficulties with the information we encounter in everyday life makes things more difficult. Therefore type design for special needs should be invisible; there is no need to emphasize the problem."

Frensch tested and analyzed the typeface throughout the developmental process, and upon completion, relied on feedback from dyslexic readers and those who teach them to gauge its effectiveness. "Tests have shown that many people, including dyslexics, have a better result while reading Read Regular," Frensch says. Perhaps the strongest evidence for the efficacy of Read Regular is its adoption for commercial use by several publishers, including Chrysalis Children's Books and Wayland Hachette Children's Books in the United Kingdom, and Uitgeverij Zwijsen and Balans Magazine in the Netherlands.

←
Read Regular designer Natascha Frensch paid close attention to the shapes of individual letters, creating noticeable differentiation by altering the stress and form of counters. This differs from many other fonts, in which letters with similar shape relationships are mirrored horizontally, making them easily transposable for readers with dyslexia.

↑
Even though each letter is treated as a unique form, Read Regular is consistent as a typeface. Frensch specifically avoided decorative features in order to stay in line with usability goals and maintain aesthetic harmony.

↓
Case Study

The North Face Tent-Pitching Instructions

Company
Satellite Design

Design Team
Amy Gustincic and Chris Harges

Client
The North Face

Audience
Outdoor enthusiasts

Pitching a Redesign

It's late, raining, and cold. The only thing louder than the howling wind is your shrieking spouse, swearing never to camp with you again. Having fun yet?

This nightmare scenario of a "fun" weekend is one of the reasons that tent designers have spent decades trying to make pitching a tent as easy as possible. Often overlooked, however, is the most crucial tool in the process: a set of clear, durable instructions.

Satellite Design faced a unique challenge when redesigning instructions for use with The North Face's tents. The client sought more effective directions, because the old instructions were text-heavy, confusing, and needlessly complex. They wanted instructions that matched their high-end, user-friendly products.

Practical Decisions
Because the instructions would be used outdoors over the long lifespan of the tent, Satellite chose a durable, synthetic paper that would withstand the rigors of repeated use in wet and/or dirty conditions. To reduce the inherent increase in unit costs, the designers reserved color for the side with the most pertinent instructions, and placed less important information in a single color on the reverse. The full-color side also included spot colors to divide instructions into three different languages.

The primary audience was obvious—tent purchasers—but the instructions were also intended for outdoor-store associates who would be using them both on the sales floor and during product clinics. "In this case, the level of knowledge and preconceived ideas about tent setup varied widely among the different audience subgroups," says designer Amy Gustincic, Co-Principal of Satellite. "It was important to address both experienced users and beginners without alienating either group."

Living the Brand
"The North Face is a premium brand," says Gustincic. "We wanted to make sure that the positive experience with the brand continued as customers interacted with their products at home." A flimsy set of instructions is a poor complement to a well-made tent. More importantly, confusing or low-quality instructions could sour a customer on The North Face brand altogether. Without the right instructions in the wilderness, the most beautifully crafted tent, costing hundreds of dollars, can easily be rendered a bad memory. Gustincic determined that the redesigned instructions must:

· *Quickly and easily walk a user through the tent setup and takedown procedure*

· *Function in low light and adverse weather conditions*

· *Last over multiple camping seasons and repeated use in adverse conditions*

· *Communicate a commitment to innovation and a focus on user-friendly design*

· *Communicate information in three languages.*

Efficient Ease
Prior to starting their design, Satellite took the time to fully understand the tent, The North Face, and its customers. They interviewed the company's tent developers and product managers, then reviewed existing instructions and competitors' instructions. They then met face to face with consumers and the outdoor-store salespeople who interface with both the clients and the instructions. They completed their

research by examining successful instruction designs for products in other markets.

This careful research provided a firm understanding of the end user's needs. Combining that information with the previously established goals for the instructions provided a recipe for design. Satellite chose color photography to clearly delineate each step. These photos illustrate, step by step, what the assembled product will look like, helping the user to understand the process at a glance. The color also makes an immediate connection to the color coding on the tent itself. The clear instructions help the user pitch the tent correctly first time, and also facilitate learning, quickly leading to a point at which the user can pitch the tent without instructions.

When the new instructions were in use, customer service complaints to The North Face about problems pitching tents decreased, clearly demonstrating a successful information design solution, and an improved experience for everyone involved.

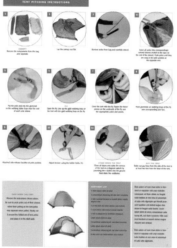

↑

Satellite Design used color photography instead of technical drawings for The North Face tent assembly instructions. This ensured that tent components were easily identified and users had a clear understanding of each step in the process. The instructions were printed on weatherproof paper, providing durability under adverse conditions.

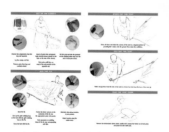

↖ ← ↙

Challenged to create a helpful, friendly set of instructions, Satellite designed and tested several different iterations, gauging their effectiveness before developing a final version. This attention to iterative design proved successful— customer complaints regarding tent instructions dropped significantly when the new instructions hit the market. Shown here are some of the early prototypes.

RiffWorks User Interface Design

Company

Scheme, LTD.

Design Team

*Lead Visual
Designer*
John-Paul Walton

*Supporting Visual
Designers*
Keith Pishnery
Dan Merk

*3-D Modeler/
Animator*
Robin Graham

Client

Sonoma Wire
Works

Audience

Amateur guitar
players

Virtual Jam Sessions

Most amateur guitarists don't have bands, audiences, or teachers to evaluate their playing. So once you've managed to work out the intro to "Stairway to Heaven," how to improve?

Sonoma Wire Works helps musicians get the feedback they need with RiffWorks, an innovative software program designed specifically for guitarists.

RiffWorks is a platform that enables guitarists to record, collaborate, and share music. The software allows them to record their riffs with whatever effects and styles they want, provides backing music to complement their guitar playing, and keeps the cost low by removing the need for physical hardware such as effects pedals or drum machines. RiffWorks also contains an online interface called RiffLink, allowing users to measure their progress or test new ideas via real-time online collaboration, easily connecting them with a community of thousands of musicians for online jam sessions—no garage necessary. Another embedded tool, RiffCaster, makes sharing work simple, providing an online forum for receiving comments and critiques. This musician-specific community simplifies the uploading process and connects guitarists directly with other players.

Beyond its interactive functionality, RiffWorks provides users with a virtual band. The software has four tempo-synchronized backups, a feature that creates backing music following the style being played. The software also provides tools that adapt sound or create unique resonance without requiring further musical hardware. In short, the software can serve as a recording device, advisor, band, critic, and music shop in one package.

RiffWorks is effective for all kinds of guitarists, even those not originally inspired by Led Zeppelin. The simple user interface is largely intuitive, and guitarists can choose between numerous styles of music (from heavy metal to country) to enhance or complement their scores. Crucially, the guitar, rather than the software, is the star of the show. Musicians can use the software to write and record music, and even create entire songs, without ever putting down their instrument.

Knowing Your Audience

RiffWorks was designed exclusively with guitarists in mind. "The original idea came from a guitar player who wanted a better way to record his riffs, so it was the classic inventor scenario of someone identifying a hole in the market based on their experiences as part of the potential audience," says John-Paul Walton, design director at Scheme, the company who designed the RiffWorks user interface, providing the look and feel of the software.

With their audience clearly identified, the design team chose to build an interface that connected playfully and intuitively. "The visual aesthetic of the interface is crucial to communicate both that this software is unique, and that we understood the audience," Walton continues. "We made the decision to convey the feeling of guitar 'gear,' which meant we were able to draw from a rich history of audio equipment design." The resulting interface mimics a guitar amplifier, right down to the incorporation of virtual knobs. The designers chose this realistic 3-D approach because it made the new product instantly familiar to its audience, and simultaneously allowed for placement of numerous controls on screen without intimidating or confusing a new user. Because most are playing largely for recreation, the software needed to be fun and easy to learn.

Making the Band

Scheme's solution required several software engineers, three designers, and an animator. The team had to work closely together as the project went from idea to fruition. The firm developed a streamlined workflow that ensured the project stayed on course, and allowed for abundant interaction internally. It also tracked all the necessary testing and revisions. The effort required to produce RiffWorks was comprehensive. Scheme provided interactive, information, and interface design as well as branding and marketing design services.

The product has fostered the same kind of cooperation among guitarists. An active and growing community of thousands of RiffWorks users post songs and collaborations online at www.sonomawireworks.com/community.php. The product struck a chord with the media, too, and RiffWorks received positive reviews in a number of major music magazines. Strong sales have led to a second version of the software, with more on the way.

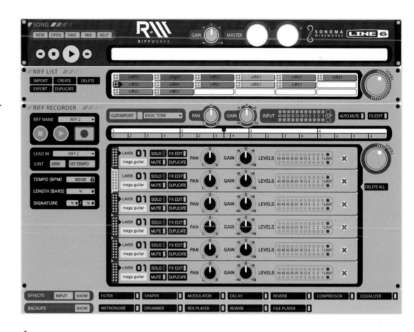

↑
The RiffWorks interface takes aesthetic cues from traditional amplifiers and effects units. This visual metaphor was used to ensure the product looked familiar to its intended audience.

↑ ↗
RiffWorks contains several studio-quality effects, allowing guitarists to add modulation, delay, reverb, and many other effects to their tunes. Aesthetic details include three-dimensional knobs and buttons, wood grain, pebbled leather, and brushed aluminum "surfaces." This attention to detail increases the accuracy of the metaphor, alluding to physical guitar gear and making the interface more approachable for the end user.

Company

Studio Panepinto,
LLC

Designer

Jennifer Panepinto

Client

Self-directed
project

Audience

Dieters and
health-conscious
individuals

An Expanding Problem

Don't tell the Western world it's getting fat. It already knows, and is constantly reminded by news reports, physicians, and government agencies.

These reminders have yet to sink in, as waistlines are growing—along with the health problems associated with obesity. Dieticians have long stressed portion control as a good way to maintain a healthy weight. The trouble is, watching portions can be cumbersome and may require extra steps when serving food.

Designer Jennifer Panepinto considered this dilemma as she ate out of a measuring cup— again. She decided that portion control could be easier and more beautiful. Through Studio Panepinto, she created Mesü, a high-end line of dishes that brings beauty and simplicity to the table for those watching their portions.

Less is More

This set of simple white bowls with colored icons representing their respective volumes start at a half-cup (118ml) portion and gradually increase in size. "With my design for Mesü," says Panepinto, "I wanted to simply show cups without saying 'cups.' When measuring cups, we refer to different sizes as quarter, half, three-quarter, etc., so it seemed natural to consider the circle as a visual representation of cups." This makes it easy to quickly identify the size of the portion, too.

The bowls stack within each other, and subtle size designations appear on the bottoms and sides of the pieces. Rather than looking like a tool for dieting, the tableware has a minimalist sensibility that would be at home in any contemporary place setting. The set carries the potential to reinforce the importance of portion control with every meal. "The hope is that it would get used continuously, unlike other diet products that get used until the novelty wears off," Panepinto offers. In addition to traditional dieters, diabetics have responded favorably to the Mesü system. The product's continued strong sales through word of mouth are a testament to its success.

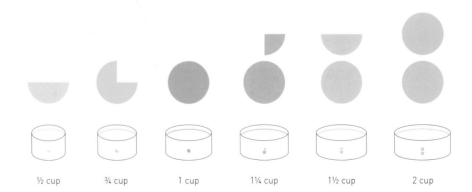

| ½ cup | ¾ cup | 1 cup | 1¼ cup | 1½ cup | 2 cup |

←←
The Mesü bowls make portion control both simple and beautiful. Understated ceramic stacking dishes imprinted with simple icons help users keep track of exactly how much they are eating. Using subdivided circles to indicate volume, the Mesü system begins with a half-cup unit (118ml), increasing in volume to two cups (473ml). This elegant design solution is functional, friendly, and sensitive to the stigma surrounding dieting.

Official Signs
& Icons 2

Company

Ultimate Symbol

Design Team

Mies Hora, working
with a large team
of designers,
production artists,
illustrators, and
consultants

Client

Self-directed
project

Audience

Environmental
and wayfinding
designers,
graphic designers,
signmakers,
governmental
and educational
institutions

Sign Language

If you've stopped at a railroad crossing, used a public restroom, or refrained from feeding bears on a camping trip, you've encountered the work of Ultimate Symbol.

Signs, symbols, and icons used in public spaces require instant clarity and accessible messages, often necessitating communication across cultural and language barriers. Many governmental entities and trade organizations require standardization of the marks used on their projects. But where does a designer go for a comprehensive and definitive resource?

Mies Hora, designer and founder of Ultimate Symbol, had this need in mind when he developed *Official Signs & Icons*. Now in its second edition, the collection gathers royalty-free vector images of thousands of signs, symbols, and icons used in wayfinding and environmental design, graphic design, architecture, and commercial publishing. The comprehensive set of digital artwork was created to meet the high standards of professional designers and includes several different collections from international standard-setting organizations.

Years In the Making

Responding to the evolving needs of the profession, Hora spent almost a decade updating the original volume of *Official Signs & Icons*—based directly on feedback from the design community. Working with design luminaries like Thomas Geismar, Paul Mijksenaar, Lance Wyman, Steff Geissbuhler, and Donald Meeker, and associations including AIGA and SEGD, Hora set out not only to catalog a collection of existing images, but also to create new systems where they were desperately needed. Three years of research and development led to the addition of a new communication system for the hospitality industry, and an updated Safety

Symbols volume connects American graphic conventions to international standards.

A Precise Process

More than just a catalog of royalty-free artwork, *Official Signs & Icons 2* offers the most accurate and useful representations possible. Hora describes the many hours spent researching, editing, and organizing. Numerous designers, production artists, and illustrators worked to digitize the collection, and all of the images included are EPS files that are resolution-independent and can be scaled and edited.

Authority Figures

The book and digitized collection have certainly hit their mark within the design community, rapidly becoming the authoritative source on the subject. As a direct result of the expertise he developed while producing *Official Signs & Icons 2*, Hora has been retained by the New York Metropolitan Transportation Authority (MTA) to provide an "iconographic assessment" of one of the most complicated

public transportation systems in the world. He is charged with evaluating the strengths and weakness in the MTA signage system, including the Long Island Rail Road, Metro North Railroad, New York City Transit (subway and buses), Long Island Bus, and Bridges & Tunnels. Hora says he has already discovered at least a dozen content messages that will require new pictograms to enhance the MTA user experience.

←
Mies Hora, founder of Ultimate Symbol, collaborated with several organizations including AIGA and SEGD to ensure that Official Signs & Icons 2 is the most comprehensive collection of icons, signs, and symbols available to the design industry. The collection was nearly a decade in the making, and was enhanced by the counsel of numerous visual professionals.

The images contained in Official Signs & Icons 2 have been painstakingly recreated as vector files so that they are resolution-independent and provide the greatest degree of flexibility to the end user.

Featuring Case Studies From:

C&G Partners

Chopping Block

Design Council

Drake Exhibits

Explanation Graphics

Futurefarmers

Inaria Brand Design
Consultants

Jazz at Lincoln Center
In-house Design

Andreas Koller and
Philipp Steinweber

LA ink

Nobel Web

Number 27

Sooy & Co.

TesisDG

White Rhino

Case Study

USPTO Museum
Exhibit Design

Company

C&G Partners

Design Team

Principal-in-Charge
Keith Helmetag

Partner Input
Steff Geissbuhler

Exhibit Designer
Fabio Gherardi

along with
numerous advisors,
fabricators, and
colleagues from
Invent Now Studio,
National Inventors
Hall of Fame
Foundation, and the
USPT Office

Client

US Patent &
Trademark Office
(USPTO) Museum

Audience

General public,
visitors to the
USPTO

Trademarks ® Cool

If the terms "patent" and "trademark" conjure up visions of dusty filing cabinets, stoic clerks, and oceans of indecipherable legal paperwork, the US Patent and Trademark Office wants to change your mind.

Looking for a way to explain their advocacy on behalf of American inventors and industry, support of technological progress and achievement, and promotion of goods and services, the US Patent and Trademark Office decided to partner with the National Inventors Hall of Fame Foundation to open a museum in their Richmond, Virginia office. They engaged with the experts at C&G Partners to find an innovative way to share their story.

On Man's Pez is Another Man's Patent
The USPTO Museum seeks to educate visitors about the critical importance of intellectual property rights in American history, and the role that the USPTO has played in protecting those rights, investing in imagination, and boosting economic development. C&G Partners worked with their client and a team of specialists to design a modular system to exhibit notable inventions and ideas. The resulting environment showcases innovation. Its grid system is uniform in size regardless of whether the medium for delivery is video, backlit film, or three-dimensional objects. This provides multiple opportunities to customize displays in the manner most appropriate to each unit's content. With consideration of the millions of patents and trademarks that have been granted, the system was designed to be scalable and easy to alter.

The resulting exhibit affords visitors an easy way to view the patents, trademarks, and, in some cases, pop-culture icons that interest them the most. Behind the simplicity is a complex array of technology. LED strips allow each display unit to customize its message, and a complex system controls lighting, sound effects, and pneumatic motion components where needed. The format of the display was determined by a readily available video monitor size, for motion graphics describing more detailed patents.

The designers were also keenly aware of developing interactive elements, creating hands-on sections of the display for visitors to interact with. Components twist, turn, and open, with an emphasis on tactile stimulus and, in some cases, even smell. These kinesthetic features help create a richer experience and take into account all of the different ways in which people can experience information.

Honoring Ideas
The inaugural exhibition was a celebration of 75 of the most interesting patents that the US Patent and Trademark Office has granted since its inception more than two centuries ago. The original installation was on display for one year, and since that time the component parts have been rearranged to create new exhibits. They will continue to be reconfigured, indefinitely, for future displays. Coincidentally, the innovative design structure created by C&G Partners was awarded its own patent by the Office.

← ↑

C&G Partners worked with the US Patent and Trademark Office Museum to create a system of interchangeable display cases featuring artifacts, motion graphics, and interactive components to tell the story of individual patents and trademarks, and the products they have inspired.

←

The display is modular, and each unit can be customized according to the needs of the museum or the requirements of the content. This image shows the complex technical system behind the exhibit wall, supporting the visitor experience.

Case Study

MoMA
What Is a Print?
Kiosk/Website

Company

Chopping Block

Design Team

Lead
Thomas Romer,
with design and
programming
support

Client

The Museum of
Modern Art (MoMA)

Audience

General public,
museum patrons,
and visitors

Art Appreciation

Most people visit art galleries to look at inspired works by famous names— rarely do they think about tools and techniques.

As a component of its curatorial efforts for a large printmaking exhibition, The Museum of Modern Art (MoMA) in New York sought to educate its visitors on the craft behind the art on display. They hired the new-media mavericks at Chopping Block to explain the process of printmaking to those who had never encountered a brayer, printing press, or jar of ink.

Learning by Doing

Thomas Romer and his design team soon recognized the benefits of creating an interactive project. They tapped into their art-school training and carefully researched the printmaking techniques with which they were less familiar. Working toward a streamlined and memorable user experience, they built storyboards for a site that would deliver large quantities of information in a compressed time frame. Built in Flash, What Is a Print? walks users through the step-by-step process of making woodcuts, etchings, lithographs, and screenprints. The site allows users to choose the print type they'd like to explore, and an interactive demonstration allows them to virtually create a print, using the selected technique, from start to finish.

Interactivity is crucial to learning and retention, says Thomas Romer, cofounder of Chopping Block. The design team actually deleted text from the project in favor of animation. Users can either watch as a print

is created, or engage in an interactive process in which their actions propel each step. Virtual printmaking becomes a memorable form of play. In less than 10 minutes, most viewers of What Is a Print? develop a good general knowledge of each technique. The site continues its educational endeavors by showcasing related fine-art examples for each process, as well a glossary and suggestions for further reading. The user leaves the What Is a Print? experience with a firm appreciation of the detailed methodology behind the works of art they are about to view.

Lasting Impressions

The project, initially commissioned as part of an on-site educational kiosk accompanying a specific printmaking exhibit, had a built-in audience of engaged observers. Due to its reception in that venue, museum officials decided to reuse the piece for any show where the work exhibited had its roots in printmaking. They also decided to place What Is a Print? on their website as an accessible outreach component of their educational programming.

This information design project is notable for its longevity and effectiveness. In the ephemeral world of the internet, What Is a Print? has remained on the MoMA site since its inception in 2001—an almost unheard-of shelf life for digital media—and continues to earn accolades. In fact, Romer says that the firm continues to reap benefits from its work for the museum, noting a number of business opportunities where the prospective client has recognized What Is a Print? in the studio's portfolio and readily engaged their services.

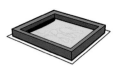

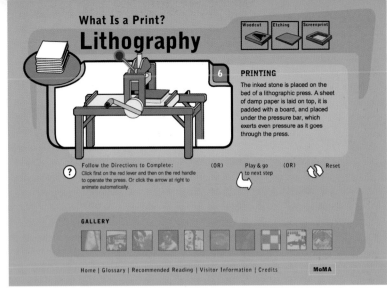

What Is a Print?
Lithography

Woodcut | Etching | Screenprint

6

PRINTING
The inked stone is placed on the bed of a lithographic press. A sheet of damp paper is laid on top, it is padded with a board, and placed under the pressure bar, which exerts even pressure as it goes through the press.

(?) Follow the Directions to Complete:
Click first on the red lever and then on the red handle to operate the press. Or click the arrow at right to animate automatically.

(OR)   Play & go to next step   (OR)   Reset

GALLERY

Home | Glossary | Recommended Reading | Visitor Information | Credits   **MoMA**

→ *This section of the What Is a Print? website describes the step-by-step process for making a screenprint. These still shots of the Flash animation show the stages a user traverses to create the final print.*

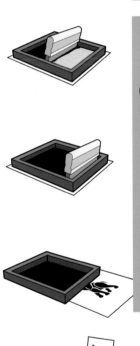

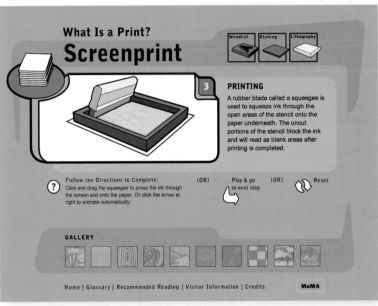

What Is a Print?
Screenprint

Woodcut | Etching | Lithography

3

PRINTING
A rubber blade called a squeegee is used to squeeze ink through the open areas of the stencil onto the paper underneath. The uncut portions of the stencil block the ink and will read as blank areas after printing is completed.

(?) Follow the Directions to Complete:
Click and drag the squeegee to press the ink through the screen and onto the paper. Or click the arrow at right to animate automatically.

(OR)   Play & go to next step   (OR)   Reset

GALLERY

Home | Glossary | Recommended Reading | Visitor Information | Credits   **MoMA**

↑ *What Is a Print? is an interactive piece used by the Museum of Modern Art in New York to educate visitors about the printmaking process. The project appears as a physical kiosk that accompanies appropriate museum exhibits, or can be viewed on the museum's website. It combines lessons in art history with interactive animations that teach the user about printmaking techniques.*

Case Study

Future Currents
Campaign

Company

Design Council

Design Team

Design Council

Client

Self-directed
project

Audience

General public,
policy makers, and
thought leaders

Personalizing a Global Problem

Man-made climate change is an established fact, yet the issue can feel so enormous and overwhelming that people feel unable to be part of a solution.

Working to alter that perception, the UK's Design Council collaborated with the London Climate Change Agency to help individuals take control of their energy use. The project, called Future Currents, focused on what individual households can do in order to change their carbon footprint. The combined effects of reduced household energy consumption have the potential to make a dramatic difference, as roughly more than a third of all greenhouse gas emissions are related to household energy use. Future Currents used a series of tools, educational materials, and financial statistics to promote energy efficiency. The effort was largely driven by a website (now archived at http://www.designcouncil.info/futurecurrents/), which proposed ideas, innovations, and services designed to reduce energy consumption. Visitors to the site were invited to join the discussion and collaborate on solutions.

The Power of Ideas

Future Currents was built on ideas, envisioning new products, services, and policies to reduce home energy consumption and carbon emissions. While almost everyone knows that leaving a light on in an empty room is wasteful, Future Currents emphasized the squander through graphics, statistics, and videos. More importantly, it proposed

viable solutions to the problem. Some were simple, others more elaborate, ranging from redesigned energy bills that utilize clear infographics to a Home Monitoring Display that shows energy use in real time for each room of a house. The proposals were often backed by statistics. In the case of the monitor, the site suggested that energy use might be reduced by as much as 15 percent if people only knew where it was going. These tangible prototypes help consumers clearly visualize the abstract notion of expending electricity or natural gas.

Future Currents categorized its solutions into four groups—Home Monitoring, Rank and Reward, Peer Power, and Hot Products—each of which offered a different way to promote conservation. Home Monitoring demonstrated effective ways to track consumption. Rank and Reward showcased financial and energy-saving incentives. Peer Power offered suggestions for homeowners to collaborate and together make greater change, often in ways that would save each household money. Hot Products featured green products from top designers that look great while minimizing energy consumption.

Inspiring Change

The Future Currents project was designed to get people thinking. Visual elements on the website were intentionally exaggerated to emphasize the message and provoke discussion. The intent of the project was not to bring each proposal to fruition, but rather to start a dialogue about the environment and how individual energy consumption and household practices have larger effects.

In 2007, the Design Council expanded and developed the ideas introduced by the Future Currents project as part of Dott (Designs of the time), a year-long series of design initiatives exploring ways in which design could make a positive difference in local communities. In particular, a project entitled Low Carb Lane explored practical ways to reduce household emissions.

Some of the ideas put forward by the Design Council's work have already made their way into the public sphere. The Greater London Assembly incorporated a number of Future Current concepts into its Green Homes initiative, including a concierge service that performs energy audits, showing homeowners how they can reduce their monthly impact, consumption, and cost—creating change one house at a time.

→ ↗
Proposed ideas are visualized, providing site visitors with clear explanations of their function. Shown here are information graphics that place personal energy consumption in context on monthly bill statements; and the project website, featuring numerous opportunities for dialogue and exchange, including a page where visitors can vote for the ideas they'd like to see happen.

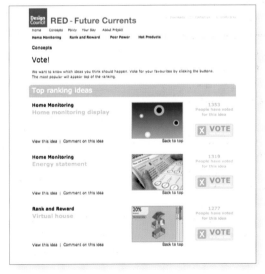

Case Study

Boston Edison
Demonstrative
Evidence

Company

Drake Exhibits

Designer

Jeff P. Drake

Client

Gibson & Behman,
Attorneys, and AIG
Insurance Company

Audience

Trial jury, judge,
and attorneys

Clear Evidence

The legal system often requires judges and juries to make major decisions based upon what they learn during a trial.

The value of design is proven time and again during litigation, as demonstrative evidence helps legal teams win cases and avoid injustice. These evidentiary exhibits make complex information accessible, often combining technical information, witness testimony, photographic evidence, scale models, and other specialized knowledge to create commonly understood materials.

Designer Jeff Drake, of Drake Exhibits, was hired to help build a case for Gibson & Behman, Attorneys and AIG Insurance as they defended a utility company—Boston Edison—from a lawsuit. The lawsuit was brought to trial by a scaffolding supervisor who claimed he was struck in the head by a pair of tin snips dropped by electricians during a refueling outage at a nuclear power plant. The defendants needed to expose inconsistencies in the plaintiff's testimony. Distilling hours of extensive research and fact-finding, Drake Exhibits produced demonstrative evidence that would do exactly that.

Systematic Inquiry

Because demonstrative evidence must be as accurate as possible to be admissible in court, it requires considerable research to produce even simple models. In the case of the tin snips accident, Drake worked with attorneys, the Occupational Safety and Health Administration, and the utility that owned

the power plant. They began by inspecting the site. After receiving training for going into the low-level radioactive environment, the team spent hours sketching, measuring, photographing, and videotaping the location of the alleged accident. They also reviewed witness depositions and building blueprints.

Drake used the gathered data to create a scale-model exhibit of the scene. He backed up his work with expert testimony based on his multidisciplinary background in fire and accident scene documentation, industrial design, architecture, graphic design, model making, and 3-D CAD modeling.

A Case for Design

Building a three-dimensional representation of this very complex accident site helped attorneys, technical experts, jury members, and the judge easily comprehend the situation. "In the demonstrative evidence field, exhibit design and execution is all about information retention," Drake explains. "Research shows that juries retain far more information through the tedious process of a trial when the evidence is presented in a concise and visually stimulating form. While not experimental in nature, the use of three-dimensional exhibits in court is still somewhat novel."

The scale model showed a figure standing where the plaintiff claimed to have been when the accident occurred. It also showed extensive scaffolding, structural elements, pipes, heating tanks, and other portions of the building. It was particularly important evidence because there were conflicting stories about the accident, and no single witness could describe exactly how it occurred. The model effectively demonstrated that it was not possible for the accident to be recreated when based upon the plaintiff's claimed location. After being introduced into evidence by the defense it was used to illustrate their case, in the courtroom, for more than a week, and the jury had further access to the model during deliberations.

The Verdict

The jury ruled in favor of the defense, finding that they were not required to pay any of the plaintiff's $9 million demand. The costs of research, design, and construction of the demonstrative evidence were minimal when compared to the staggering return on investment they produced for the client. And the model's function didn't end with the court case. After the appeals process ended, it was given to the Pilgrim Station nuclear power plant for use in training maintenance personnel.

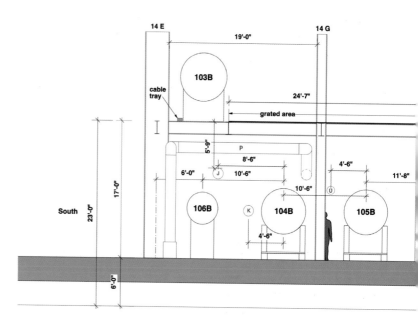

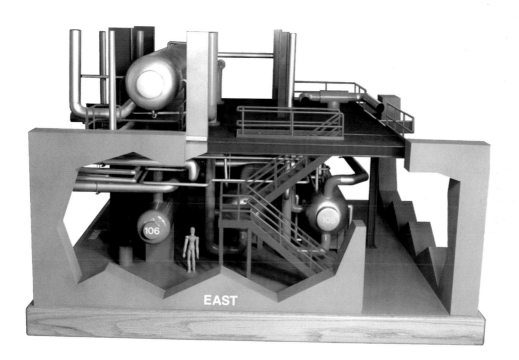

↑
After low-level radiation training, investigators, including Drake, had full access to the accident site. Diagrams like this were created from hands-on measurements, photography, and video, establishing a guide for building a scale model of the area.

←
Site inspection and expert consultation aided the creation of this model for the defendant of a $9 million lawsuit. The plaintiff claimed that he had been hit on the head with a tool dropped from above. Drake Exhibits' research, and the resulting model, helped prove that the situation described in the plaintiff's testimony was not possible.

Company

Explanation Graphics

Design Team

Nigel Holmes and Rowland Holmes

Client

Technology, Entertainment, Design (TED) Conference

Audience

TED Conference attendees and the general public

Facts You Can't Ignore

A trillion of anything is a staggering sum. Even if you're a math nerd and know it is a million million, or a 1 followed by 12 zeroes, the number might be difficult to comprehend in practical terms.

This is one of many reasons why the US national debt is out of sight and out of mind for many American citizens. With the national debt way past the $1 trillion mark, and spending continuing to rise, designer Nigel Holmes and web producer Rowland Holmes of Explanation Graphics sought to deliver a widely accessible message that put the magnitude of the debt into a recognizable context. Using their own research, they developed a short graphic movie that placed the figure in relation to familiar objects.

Delivering Meaning from Numbers

Using the slender thickness of a $100 bill, Homes built stacks representing a recent US government surplus and the current national debt. The filmmakers then compared those stacks to the height of a person, the Empire State Building, and finally Mount Everest. As the film illustrates, the surplus, which was in the billions, is quickly dwarfed by the deficit, which stretches for thousands of miles into outer space.

The movie was created for the Technology, Entertainment, Design (TED) conference, which offers a platform for the most innovative and creative thinkers in the world to share their ideas. The conference presents speakers with a challenge: to deliver "the talk of their lives" in 18 minutes. Explanation Graphics employed humor and fun to tell an important story in a compressed time frame. Despite the intellectual slant of the conference itself, the resulting design piece is accessible to anyone, regardless of their level of education.

The film uses simple animation and well-paced explanatory narration to produce an important and lasting effect. In five minutes, a trillion is transformed from an abstract—and possibly incomprehensible—number to an unbelievably vast amount, demanding thought and action.

→

This series of screenshots from the movie The Surplus and the Debt *by Explanation Graphics shows how simple information graphics, when paired with animation and wit, make an extremely complex topic easy to understand.*

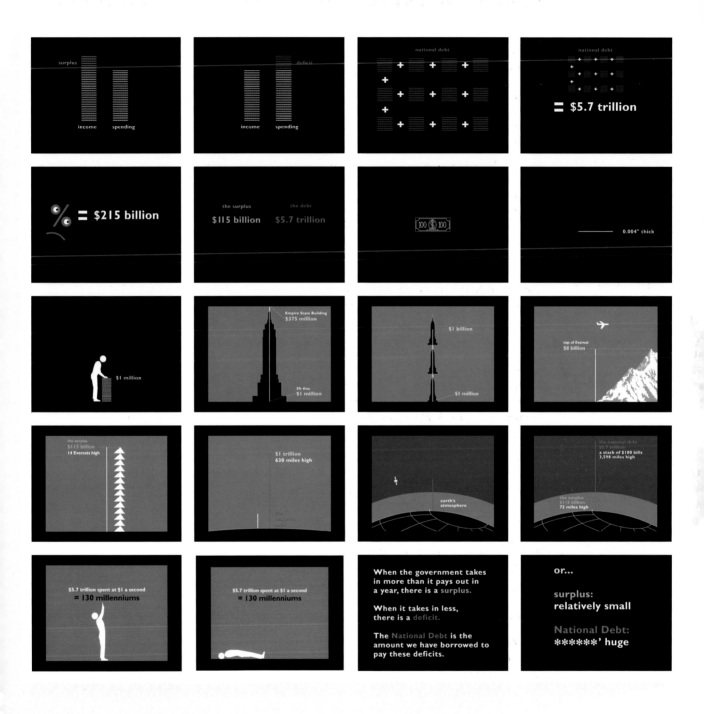

Company

Explanation
Graphics

Designer

Nigel Holmes

Client

Sports Illustrated
Magazine

Audience

Subscribers and
sports fans

Tracking the Tour

Explaining the rigors of the Tour de France in a roughly 2 × 9in (5 × 23cm) magazine graphic may seem extreme.

Perhaps *Sports Illustrated*, a weekly magazine with a principally US readership, had that in mind when they contacted designer Nigel Holmes of Explanation Graphics, giving him just two days to develop a graphic that would convey the highlights of the Tour (which was about halfway complete at press time). Using research provided by the magazine, as well as his own, Holmes made a graphic map of the race showing the distances and elevations of each stage, as well as crashes, transitions, locales, and other information. In a compressed space, Holmes manages to illustrate the most challenging stages (with a graph-like elevation scale) while using pithy prose to concisely explain the race, its trials, and its grand victories. The graphic complemented the accompanying article, and helped give readers an insight into the dramatic distance and elevation gains during the three-week race.

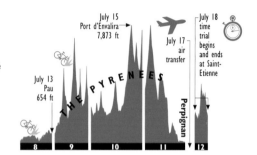

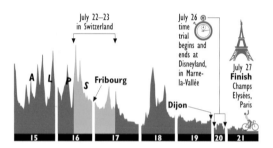

↓ ↑ ↑ ↑

Although small, this information graphic designed by Nigel Holmes has a very dense information resolution. Covering 2,403 miles (3,867km) in just nine inches (23cm), the graphic communicates the most relevant information about

the Tour de France, including distance, elevation change, location, crashes, and individual stage information.

Details above shown at 100%.

TOUR DE FORCE
Cyclists are about halfway through the three weeks of the Tour de France. 198 riders started from Rouen on July 5 (the route is different each year); 19 are already out of the race with injuries. Here are the peaks and valleys of their 2,403-mile ride, compressed into nine inches.

● One stage per day
● The 19 road stages range in length from 92 to 163 miles
● Crashes through July 14

↓
Case Study

GOOD Magazine
"Transparency"
Feature

Company

Futurefarmers

Designer

Amy Franceschini

Client

GOOD Magazine

Audience

Subscribers

Bringing Life to Data

An Excel spreadsheet may excite an accountant, but delivering data for a demanding audience like the readers of *GOOD* Magazine requires a creative approach.

GOOD subscribers tend to be highly educated, and are often engaged in a creative field.

The magazine approached designer Amy Franceschini of Futurefarmers, a San Francisco agency, to design infographics for the magazine. *GOOD* covers a huge variety of issues, but its central mission is to drive change through the exchange of ideas. It tackles topics ranging from homelessness to sustainability to economics. The core theme: present new ideas, stimulate thought, and inspire action.

Franceschini produced infographics for the magazine's "Transparency" feature. Using data from Excel spreadsheets provided by researchers at *GOOD*, she created rich visuals that not only deliver the required information, but do so with flair and whimsy.

Graphing a New Course

Though simple graphs are a staple for magazines, Franceschini approached the medium creatively. To demonstrate the vastness of certain popular American retailers, she illustrated the number of stores with a traditional bar-graphing technique, but added depth to those numbers by illustrating the respective retailers' footprints within the graph. This allows the viewer to easily see that, for example, while there are more

Starbucks coffee concessions in the US than Blockbuster Video stores, the video stores take up more square mileage due to their size. The power of the graph is most striking when looking at the Wal-Mart effect: the retail giant's footprint dwarfs that of any of its fellow retailers. In fact, the total area of Wal-Mart stores throughout the US is approaching 30 square miles (77.6km^2), which is roughly equivalent in size (the viewer learns) to the island of Manhattan.

Similarly, Franceschini's illustration of student debt in the US provides a stunning look at a rapidly growing problem. The designer chose to interpret the ballooning problem quite literally—with a series of hot-air balloons, each representing a calendar year of steadily increasing debt. Below the balloon illustration, important statistics support critical consideration of the issue.

Strong Messages

Franceschini employed striking visuals and key facts to present sets of information on solar energy and American sugar consumption.

The sugar graphic focuses on the growing popularity of soft drinks during the past 30 years. The consequences are implied by creating a bulging can of soda overlaid by a sugar spoon. Franceschini's clean typography overlaying the graphic delivers the key research findings, supported by additional text and graphics below.

The solar energy layout uses an eye-catching rainbow palette that mirrors the spectrum of visible light. Compelling facts about solar energy and its potential are delivered alongside scientific details and kitschy graphics warning the reader not to look directly at the sun. The result is a quickly read and easily digested nugget of varied information.

→↘
Franceschini uses bold graphic shapes and bright colors to communicate information about American sugar consumption and the energy produced by the sun. Whimsical images are supported by data sets, providing a hybrid editorial and infographic solution.

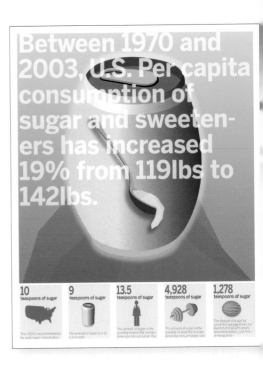

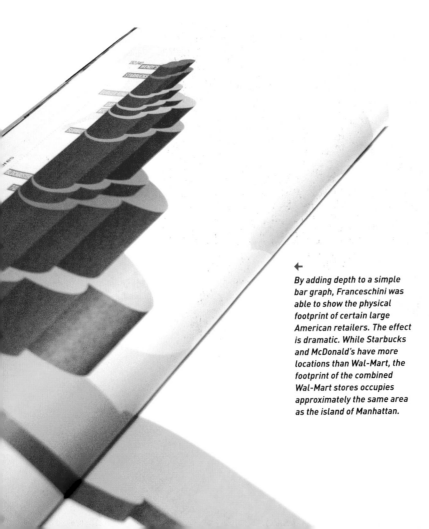

←
By adding depth to a simple bar graph, Franceschini was able to show the physical footprint of certain large American retailers. The effect is dramatic. While Starbucks and McDonald's have more locations than Wal-Mart, the footprint of the combined Wal-Mart stores occupies approximately the same area as the island of Manhattan.

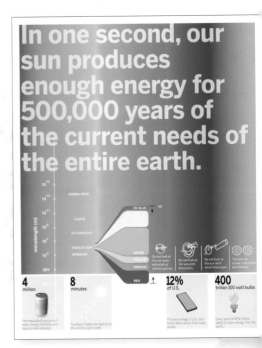

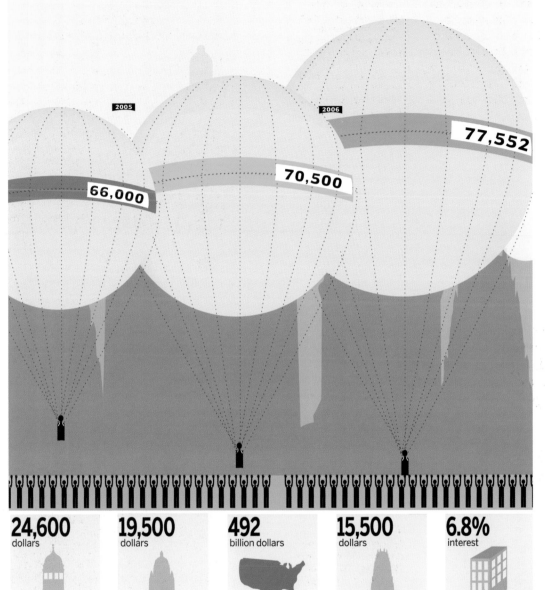

2005

2006

66,000

70,500

77,552

Franceschini's chart demonstrating student debt in the US illustrates the problem with a sequence of hot-air balloons, each representing a calendar year of steadily increasing debt.

24,600
dollars

Median debt from for-profit colleges.

19,500
dollars

Median debt from private, non-profit colleges.

492
billion dollars

The total amount of U.S. student debt.

15,500
dollars

Median debt from public, four year college.

6.8%
interest

The interest rate on federal student loans.

Company

Inaria Brand Design
Consultants

Design Team

Creative Director
Andrew Thomas

Designer
Andrew Thomas

Illustration
Paul Davis

Client

Xtreme Information

Audience

Decision makers
at FTSE 100 and
Fortune 500
multinational
companies, media
and advertising
agencies

Streamlining Communication

Designers like to joke that no one reads copy. Like most humor, the statement contains some truth, particularly as our lives become busier.

Xtreme Information, a company specializing in media and competitive intelligence, needed to reach potential clients. However, explaining their 13 products and four key markets was not a "quick read." The company wanted to demystify its sophisticated suite of analytical services. To do so, they enlisted brand design consultants Inaria to deliver a compelling and expeditious snapshot of their offerings.

Complex Doesn't Mean Complicated

As the world's largest media-intelligence company, Xtreme Information provides numerous services through 13 separately branded product lines. Each one gives clients access to multiple types of competitive intelligence, from tools like Xtreme ADX, which calculates competitors' advertising expenditure across multiple media channels, to The Reel, which profiles the best in television advertising and identifies the agencies responsible for the campaigns. Each service is exceedingly technical in nature. Xtreme already had a complex website and brochures describing each of its products. But all of that detailed information didn't help them deliver the concise "elevator pitch" needed for targeting new business development. Hence, Inaria focused on creating a single, easily absorbed message. Their challenge was to find the similarities in each of Xtreme's service offerings, creating a leave-behind that showcased the value of the firm's capabilities.

Inaria determined that while the client's offerings were complex, they essentially told a single story: "Xtreme offers the knowledge you need to have a competitive advantage in your marketplace." To support this message, they developed a conceptual structure for the brochure they were creating: Vision + Knowledge = Intelligence. The "Vision" section explains in basic terms what Xtreme does, demonstrating the value of their services and asking potential customers to imagine what Xtreme might offer them. "Knowledge" delineates the unique merits of each product line, helping the reader understand the benefits of their proprietary technology. "Intelligence" reinforces the competitive advantages that Xtreme's products provide, and shows potential clients how to select tools that suit their specific needs.

The design team envisioned a corporate overview brochure, but eschewed the ephemeral qualities of saddle stitching and glossy stock photography in favor of producing a beautifully illustrated hard-bound book, the content of which could be understood by a completely cold prospect or an eager client. They resolved to keep copy concise, and worked with renowned illustrator Paul Davis to create simple line drawings that would allude to sketching and idea development. These were augmented with screenshots, charts, graphs, and photographs of magazine spreads to delineate the benefits of Xtreme's numerous services.

Message Received

The resulting document captured the essence of the organization and helped explain Xtreme's value proposition in an exciting, user-centric manner. Many of Xtreme's clients keep the document as a reference tool for future service offerings. The company continues to update and reprint the book, and strongly praise Inaria for their approach. "What we asked for was a corporate brochure, what Inaria gave us was a beautifully crafted book which has won us business and elevated our status in the marketplace," says Xtreme Information CEO John Gordon. "We moved from being just suppliers to partners in the provision of global media intelligence. Outstanding!"

By designing an elegant and approachable book that uses handwritten text and illustrated graphics to explain technical service offerings, Inaria demystified their client's products and helped them showcase their capabilities.

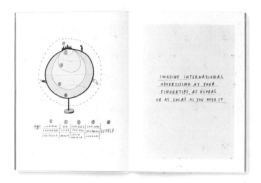

Case Study

JALC
Subscription
Campaign

Company

Jazz at Lincoln
Center In-house
Design

Design Team

Design Director
Bobby C. Martin Jr.

Senior Designer
Matthew Poor Jr.

Designer
Erika Lee

Client

Jazz at Lincoln
Center

Audience

Subscribers and
new customers,
jazz novices and
aficionados

A New Tune

As one of the world's preeminent music venues, Jazz at Lincoln Center (JALC) hosts an event or performance—often more than one—almost every night of the year.

With all that programming comes a massive need for information design. When the organization developed collateral for its subscription campaign, it knew the materials would be delivering a lot of content, but they also needed to look the part. Jazz has a strong visual history, almost as vibrant and exciting as the music itself. The JALC design team wanted to do more than present concert details and performer biographies—they wanted to create a new visual language for the season, striving to communicate the emotional experience of attending a performance.

Generating Excitement

As an organization with a sophisticated and upscale clientele, Jazz at Lincoln Center wanted to create materials that patrons would be likely to keep. The designers stretched themselves, striving to create something memorable. "Even a brochure is interactive," says designer Matthew Poor. "You touch it, fold it, keep it with you, pin it on your fridge. Nice paper; bright, bold ink; and a consistent commitment to excellent printing all help people want to keep your pieces. A flyer someone takes home is the best retention we could hope for." Jazz at Lincoln Center relies heavily on repeat business, and revenue depends on current patrons and potential clients having easy access to all the details of its event calendar.

The team chose a large format for the subscription campaign's print work, and selected bright colors and graphics to convey the exuberance and intensity of a jazz show. While evocative, the pieces still had to deliver concert and calendar information, performance details, and other content in an easy-to-access manner. They established detailed grids and typographic systems to cleanly organize content, pairing the delivery with hip copywriting. They understood the importance of clear navigation, emphasizing clear focal points and good visual hierarchy, while engaging the reader with color and imagery.

A High Note

The designers had access to a wealth of knowledge to inform their aesthetic decisions. Jazz at Lincoln Center has extensive data on its audience's demographics and habits, so they were able to target their message directly at the end recipient. Beyond the numbers, the designers worked with musicians and considered the historical context of jazz while developing the collateral. The net result is a fresh take on a decades-old American art form, one that delivers information in a simple and distinctive fashion. The design team's thoughtful efforts have paid off—the center has seen a 60 percent increase in ticket sales, and an increase of approximately 120 percent in membership enrollment.

→

Clear hierarchy is essential for organizing copious amounts of information. The design team at Jazz at Lincoln Center was charged with structuring concert dates, musicians' biographies, event descriptions, and subscription forms, while simultaneously creating a seasonal brand image—all on one piece of paper.

Company

N/A

Design Team

Andreas Koller and
Philipp Steinweber

Client

Self-directed
project

Audience

General public

Common Conviction

In an era of increasingly divisive religious conflict and debate, we've heard peacemakers expound on the fundamental shared beliefs of world religions.

But with tensions on the rise, designers Andreas Koller and Philipp Steinweber felt that the message was often falling on deaf ears. The pair were working under the direction of Stefan Sagmeister during his professorship in Salzburg, Austria. They undertook the challenge to visually demonstrate the overlap between the main holy texts of Buddhism, Christianity, Hinduism, Islam, and Judaism. Their project, Similar Diversity, is a large-scale graphic representation of a digitized text analysis, comparing like content within the selected holy books and scriptures on a word-by-word basis.

A Call to Reason

Religion is an inherently personal topic, so Koller and Steinweber sought to remove all subjectivity from their approach. Their multicolored chart is purely informational; the pair used the node-based programming tool VVVV and the open-source programming language Processing to help gather and organize data. With these tools, they analyzed nearly three million words, selecting the 41 most frequently referenced names/characters and their associated "activities" (verbs linked to the character's name). The resulting informational display is presented in a large format, approximately 10ft tall by 23ft long (3 × 7m). Viewers must literally walk through

the diagram to study its results. And while it is a gathering and alignment of quantifiable content, the information graphic also often elicits a strong emotional response, inspiring thought and analysis.

How It Works

The designers alphabetically arranged the names of the holy characters in a horizontal line. Those names were sized based on their total word count across all the reviewed scriptures and texts, making "God," "Lord," and "You" the largest words. Above each name is a multicolored arc, each segment representing a religion. The length of the segments corresponds directly with the frequency of the word's appearance in that religion's respective document(s). Below each name is a column of words. These are the verbs most frequently occurring in connection with that character's name, ordered from top (most commonly used) to bottom (least commonly used). The row for each verb is color-segmented in the same fashion; its height varies according to percentage of use. These structural decisions defined the cast of characters.

→

Similar Diversity is designed to be part of a physical environment. The level of detail and the complexity of the project dictate a large format. The impact of studying the graphic in an open space provides a communal experience and offers common ground for conversation.

Bhikkhu • Brahman • Buddha • David • Devi • Elijah • God • Indra

↑
Similar Diversity is an installation-sized information graphic that shows the overlap between characters and actions in the holy books of five world religions: Buddhism, Christianity, Hinduism, Islam, and Judaism.

An array of gray arches soaring above the characters at varying heights and thicknesses visualizes connectivity. The weight and opacity of each connecting arc was determined by an algorithm that compared similarities between the activities of pairs of characters. The character pairs with the most in common are represented by the darkest, thickest arcs. This allows the viewer to selectively compare likeness of language and action.

Provocative Connections

Similar Diversity strips away interpretive passages, simply connecting subjects and verbs and highlighting common occurrences. This clinical analysis of language avoids the contention of religious debate. Yet the very nature of the subject being studied connects with the viewer on an emotional level, its visual clarity forcing some to reconsider long-held opinions. The project has won praise for its categorical display of commonality in a discordant social era.

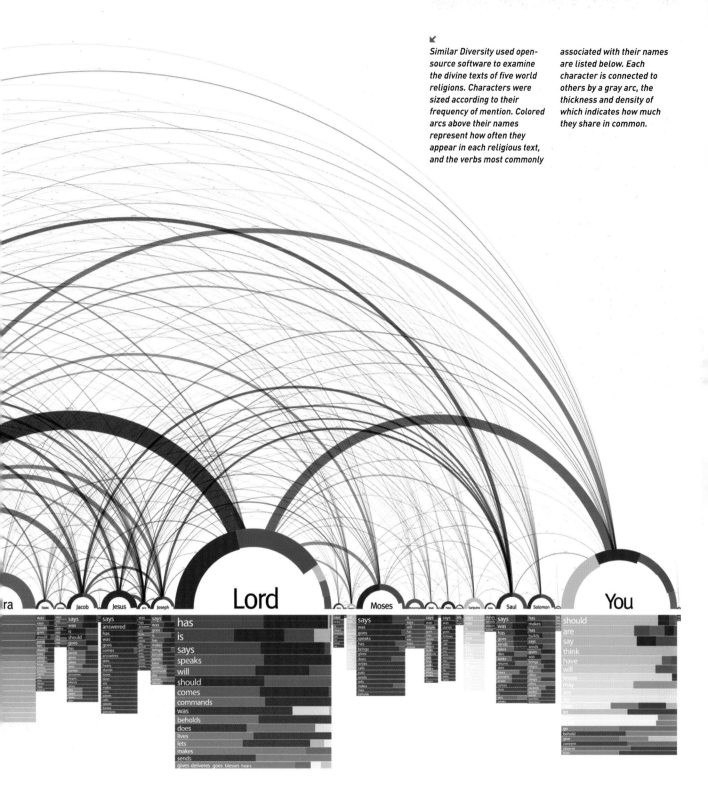

Similar Diversity used open-source software to examine the divine texts of five world religions. Characters were sized according to their frequency of mention. Colored arcs above their names represent how often they appear in each religious text, and the verbs most commonly associated with their names are listed below. Each character is connected to others by a gray arc, the thickness and density of which indicates how much they share in common.

Case Study

Wall of
Discovery

Company

LA ink

Design Team

Drew Sternal and
Joseph Olson

Client

University of
Minnesota

Audience

The University
of Minnesota
community
(administrators,
faculty, students,
alumni, etc.)

Broad Scope Comes into Focus

Few places better exemplify the many facets of the human spirit than a college campus.

A university's central mission of education encompasses research, communication, art, recreation, interaction, and more. Successfully representing such a wide range of content in a large-scale graphic format presented a challenge for LA ink, a Minneapolis-based design firm, when it was tasked with creating a way to honor the achievements of distinguished alumni of the University of Minnesota.

Working with an architectural firm, LA ink helped create the Wall of Discovery, a 253ft (77.1m) outdoor tribute to learning, innovation, and creativity. The wall is a concluding element to the Scholars Walk project, which recognizes top University of Minnesota-connected achievers in science, academia, literature, and other fields. The combined elements are prominently placed on the university's main Minneapolis campus.

Art, Science, and Design Merge

Rather than building a simple mural, the design team conceived a large-scale simulated blackboard, covered with oversized theories, sketches, ideas, and formulas by the university's great thinkers. They paired this with 20 large illuminated glass panels that provoke both literal and figurative reflection from the viewer. Together, the blackboard and glass celebrate the achievements of the past while encouraging viewers to consider the future. "It simultaneously commemorates the work of the university and inspires young minds," says

designer Drew Sternal. "The juxtaposition of the two elements is important. The blackboard is largely a record of the past, those thought processes and enlightened breakthroughs that now inform our world, whereas the illuminated glass panels are doorways to inspiration which invite us to contemplate the future."

New Ideas Every Visit

While people directly tied to the university are the main audience, everyone in the state has a connection, because it is a public school. That said, LA ink recognized that the Wall of Discovery would be a part of the campus, and be seen multiple times by students, faculty, and others. "In terms of design," says Sternal, "the Wall of Discovery is meant to be endlessly fascinating. It is not meant to be readily understood and fully consumed in a short period of time." Included in the wall are complex formulas and theories that, interestingly, may become clearer to students as they continue on their journey toward graduation. As such, the wall is a dynamic place, where previously unrecognized ideas may come to life over the course of many visits. Sternal says that most first-time visitors spend 10–30 minutes looking at the wall, but viewers who see it frequently often note that they find something new each time.

The experience itself is not the only element designed to change. LA ink planned the Wall of Discovery on the understanding that it would need to be updated as new scholars earned their place in the university's history.

Research Makes Design Come Alive

To bring the design to life, LA ink developed a comprehensive list of scholarly achievements by University of Minnesota faculty and students. From that list, they sought to obtain as many unique, handwritten documents as possible from the scholars' archives. Because more than half of the acquisitions came from sources outside the university, and all required permission for use, it was a long and challenging research project. A great deal of time was spent verifying each entry's accuracy and origins.

LA ink scanned each acquisition at a very high resolution for use in the large-scale project, retouching to remove all traces of the medium on which it was authored. The final blackboard art was created digitally, and allows for frequent and economical updates—an ideal solution for a display dedicated to continual learning.

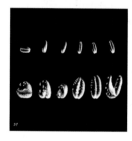

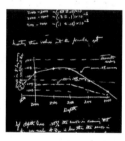

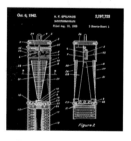

↗ ↗

The Wall of Discovery, part of Scholars Walk at the University of Minnesota, is a beautiful exhibit of world-class scholarship displayed for all to see. Viewers have the opportunity to explore the sketches, formulas, diagrams, and profound scribblings of leading thinkers who graduated from, or taught at, the university. These are the beginnings of miraculous inventions, cures, and processes that continue to influence our world.

↖

Detail: Alexander Anderson, PhD, BS Botany 1894, MS Botany 1895, Assistant Professor of Botany.

Notes and sketches on the cereal grain puffing process. Anderson eventually received 25 patents on the puffing process and the machinery used to manufacture it.

↖ ↑

Detail: Athelstan Spilhaus, PhD, Dean of the Institute of Technology 1949–66.

Personal notes, calculations, and patent drawings for the bathythermograph, an instrument that became standard equipment on all US Navy submarines and vessels involved in antisubmarine warfare.

Case Study

Nobel Prize
Interactive
Games

Company

Nobel Web

Design Team

Karin Svanholm,
Agneta Wallin
Levinovitz, with
animators,
illustrators,
programmers,
scriptwriters, and
subject-based
external experts

Client

Nobel Foundation

Audience

English-speaking
teenagers

Reaching a New Audience

You're 14 years old, and presented with a choice: listen to a lecture about a Nobel Prize-winning scientist, or play a video game. How long did it take you to decide?

The design team at the Nobel Foundation knew the answer, and decided to bring their message to a more attractive medium.

The Nobel Prize is internationally recognized as the pinnacle of professional, artistic, or political achievement. The prize has brand-name recognition, and most adults appreciate the talent, innovation, and creativity that goes into the projects honored by the Nobel Foundation. But how well recognized would the Nobel name be to future generations? To ensure continued support for its mission to recognize the efforts that most benefit mankind each year, the foundation needed to extend its outreach to a younger audience.

The Importance of Education

The Nobel Foundation established an Educational Outreach Program to introduce its illustrious prizewinners to a new generation. Seeking to reinforce the importance of arts and sciences, and the ongoing quest for peace, they focused on the needs of middle-school and high-school children. As part of this effort, the foundation created a series of interactive educational games based on the six categories of Nobel Prizes—Chemistry, Economics, Literature, Medicine, Physics, and Peace. The designers knew their audience was looking

for entertainment, and decided to extend their message through games, experiments, and simulations that any online audience could access and explore.

Learning by Doing

Written in English, the most widely used language on the internet, the games impart a variety of educational information through the use of simple interactivity. Created in Flash, they are accessible to anyone who downloads a free plugin. Games usually take about 5 to 20 minutes to complete, depending on the complexity of the subject and the user's skill and level of engagement. Each is preceded by a detailed explanation of the prizewinner and subject upon which the game is based, so readers have access to more detailed information than may be delivered during play. The design team performs user testing on all the games before they are released to the public. They observe teenaged test-players in pairs, and interview them afterward in order to better understand their target audience's interests, abilities, likes, and dislikes.

Examples include a medical game featuring an emergency-room setting where the player must assess an accident victim's blood type and determine what can safely be used for transfusion. In order to successfully complete the task, the player must understand the basic principles of blood typing. In another game, supporting the Nobel Peace Prize, the goal is to disarm the world's nuclear weapons. Factoids about nuclear states are delivered in a question-and-answer format, and the player must correctly identify all of the countries to complete the mission. A literature-themed game features that staple of teenage libraries, *Lord of the Flies*. This game is meant to be played after reading the book, and helps emphasize the symbolism in the story.

Nobelprize.org's educational games have enjoyed a surprisingly long shelf life for digital work (some were designed in 2001), and are only removed from the site if the design team feels they've become too dated, or changes in browser technology can no longer support their function. Their popularity is driving traffic to the foundation's website, and the design team credits the games with a 60 percent increase in visitors between 2006 and 2007. The educational games use play to showcase how Nobel Laureates' innovations affect the world and our daily experience, helping to ensure the relevance and vitality of the foundation's important work for years to come.

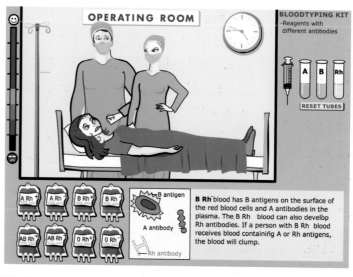

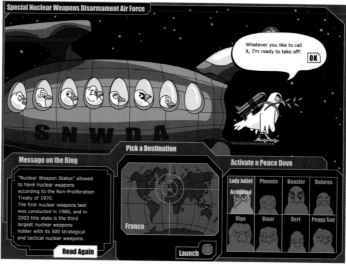

↗ ↗ →

A series of fun and informative educational games are available to the general public at nobelprize.org. The website provides interactive gaming experiences for each of its prize categories: Chemistry, Economics, Literature, Medicine, Physics, and Peace.

The screenshots shown here are from:

Blood Typing, *which places teens in a virtual ER, teaching*

them the basics of blood typing to save accident victims, encouraging a future interest in medicine.

Peace Doves, *a game created to educate kids about nuclear disarmament. Players send peace doves on a mission to disarm each of the eight countries that possess nuclear weapons.*

Details from both games are also shown.

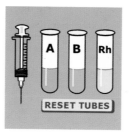

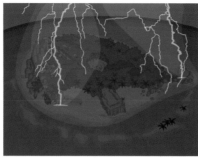

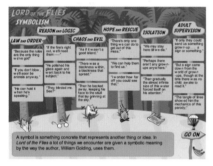

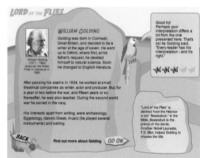

↑
The Lord of the Flies *game
is built around William
Golding's novel of the same
name. Intended for use
after a student has read the
book, it takes players on an
interactive journey through
the story, emphasizing its
symbolism.*

Company

Number 27

Designer

Jonathan Harris

Client

Self-directed
project

Audience

Internet users

The Human Touch

Conventional thinking says that, while technology can make our lives easier, it often isolates us.

While the internet has opened countless opportunities and broken many communication barriers, it is often perceived as an anonymous tool, used by anonymous individuals. In short, it helps people talk at each other, but rarely seems to help people communicate with one another.

Much of Jonathan Harris's work at his Number 27 studio is dedicated to rejecting the modern cliché of a cold, uncaring internet. Harris's projects often seek to dispel the notion that the internet is a dehumanizing medium which separates and isolates people. Instead, Harris combines customized web software with a flair for whimsy to design interactive projects that reveal and celebrate human emotion and stimulate creativity online. Harris built the sites discussed here not for any client, but to satisfy his own interests and curiosity.

"Most of my projects start with simple questions that I ask myself about the world," Harris explains. "Then I typically think about ways to answer those questions using large sets of online data."

Unconventional Thinking

Jonathan Harris takes his ideas and collaborates with server expert Sep Kamvar to develop methods of constantly aggregating, analyzing, and assembling reams of online data. Rather than presenting the data conventionally, which might be dry or overwhelming, Harris develops clever and engaging methods that remind visitors to his sites that the internet is an assembly of humanity rather than a technological behemoth. Harris's sites encourage interaction and provide a glimpse

into the lives of others through simple ideas that are executed brilliantly. At once playful and serious, trivial and profound, Harris's work is exceptional proof that the way data is presented matters as much as the data itself.

Taking Data, Making Stories

We'll examine three Harris-designed sites as case studies: Lovelines (love-lines.com), We Feel Fine (wefeelfine.org), and WordCount (wordcount.org). All three sites encourage the audience to play, interact, and interpret data. The sites also share stories that viewers can read, add to, or invent.

How it Works

To pull content for Lovelines and We Feel Fine, a system searches thousands of English-language blog entries every few minutes for occurrences of certain phrases: "I feel" and "I am feeling" for We Feel Fine, and "I love/I like/I want/I don't want/I don't like/I don't love/I hate" for Lovelines. The back-end computer program also captures any demographic data that is available, such as gender, location, age, or even weather. But that is just the technical side. Harris presents the data in a way that makes the information part of a dynamic, user-driven, interactive art display.

"Realizing these projects online ensures they are never 'finished,' but instead constantly grow and change with new content, reflecting the changing landscape of human emotion and desire," Harris elaborates.

Choose Your Experience

In We Feel Fine, Harris assigns various colors to different emotions, creating floating specks on a field of black. In this applet, users can group data in a variety of ways, look at individual sentences, photos, and stories, and even link to the original blog posts themselves.

The result is a data-driven snapshot of the world's emotions.

"In We Feel Fine, all those colored particles exhibit human traits like curiosity, fright, euphoria, and nomadicism," Harris says. "But they can also be asked to self-organize along any number of axes, coalescing into maps, charts, and graphs that provide various statistical insights into the world's feelings. It is this sense of micro and macro working together (many stories forming statistics, and statistics disintegrating into their constituent stories) that makes We Feel Fine successful."

Choose Your Emotion

Lovelines locates and displays sentences containing "I love" or expressing other feelings or desires. The site also finds such phrases attached to photographs. Site users can view either photographs with phrases or just the phrases themselves; all are linked to the original sources. Users can also select the type of phrases they see by using a sliding scale on the page that moves between the extremes of love and hate.

"These projects are not so much meant to be learning tools as they are meant to provide short, sometimes irretrievable glimpses into the headspace of other humans," Harris continues. "It is not often that we get to glimpse strangers in these private moments."

Choose your Interpretation

Wordcount takes a list of the most frequently used words in English, provided by the British National Corpus, and generates a simple visualization. Harris displays the 86,800 words in alternating gray and black, side by side, as a very long sentence: "The project was designed to bring a playful quality to an otherwise dry list of data."

The manner in which the information is presented has produced some surprises, according to Harris: "Interactivity is an important part of what allows this word-frequency data to come to life. Games have emerged, where people try to find sequences of words in Wordcount that form apparently conspiratorial phrases like 'america ensure oil opportunity,' 'microsoft acquire salary tremendous,' and 'construction ahead.'"

Built to Last

Harris creates his sites with simple, intuitive interfaces to make them easy to use, encourage interaction, and ensure that the sites won't look dated as they continue to change over time. "The projects are never 'done'—they are designed to keep on growing as long as people keep blogging." Each of Harris's sites has a timeless quality due to its use of clean fonts, minimal graphics, and basic backgrounds.

Defining Success

Harris has cast a wide net with these projects and plays a dual role as creator and client—a luxury few designers enjoy. There is much to learn from Harris's exploration of unframed problems, and his innovative approach to presenting information, inspiring interaction, and reminding a data-obsessed world that design is a powerful force.

→
Every few minutes, We Feel Fine gathers information from recently posted blog entries that contain the phrases "I feel" and "I am feeling." The system then records the full sentence up to the period; identifies the feeling; and documents age, gender, geographic location, and even weather conditions. The We Feel Fine database now stores several million feelings, with up to 20,000 added each day.

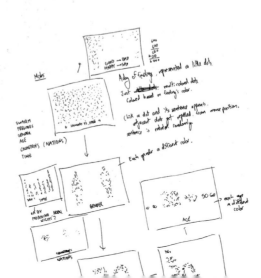

←
Jonathan Harris's developmental sketch for one of the We Feel Fine movements showcases both its graphic and structural concepts.

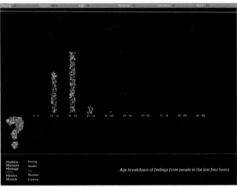

Feeling breakdown of feelings from people aged 20 to 29

Age breakdown of feelings from people in the last few hours

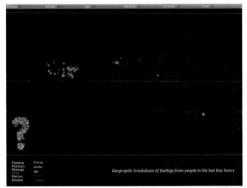

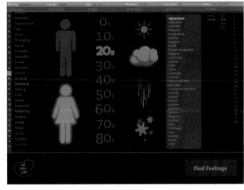

Geographic breakdown of feelings from people in the last few hours

→ →

We Feel Fine allows the user to aggregate information based on six different "movements": Madness, Murmur, Montage, Mobs, Metrics, and Mounds. In the following examples:

Murmur presents the data as structured sentences that scroll down from the top of the screen.

Montage presents entries that also contain an associated photograph.

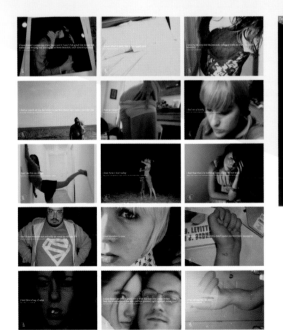

Using the same data-collection engine as We Feel Fine, Lovelines sifts through blog entries every few minutes looking for expressions of love and hate. The entry is then positioned on a sliding scale according to the strength of the emotion. Users can view the collection through portals of Words, Pictures, or Superlatives, as well as confine the data by month and year.

WordCount ranks the order of 86,800 of the most frequently used words in the English language. Each is sized according to use: the larger the word, the more often it is used.

One result that Harris did not forecast is that many WordCount users hunt for meanings in coincidental sequences of words, sometimes finding phrases like this: "america ensure oil opportunity."

Company

Sooy & Co.

Designer

Brian Sooy

Client

Tyndale House
Publishers

Audience

Bible readers,
specifically a target
demographic of
ages 30–50

One Important Client

When's the last time you chose a font based on its ergonomic and economic impact?

Typographic decisions are often based on aesthetics or style. But when Tyndale House Publishers was choosing a font for the second edition of its best-selling *New Living Translation Bible*, it had a lot more to consider. First, the text had to be comfortable and easy on the eyes of readers in their target demographic of ages 30–50. Secondly, Tyndale was facing increases in printing, paper, and ink costs—so a font that could achieve a better character count would save them a lot of money.

Although Tyndale had several off-the-shelf options, Brian Sooy of Sooy & Co. had been discussing the advantages of a custom typeface with Timothy Botts, senior art director at Tyndale, for a number of years. Sooy was ultimately commissioned to produce Lucerna. He was designing for a version of the Bible that had been translated with the goal of making it easier to read and understand for a modern audience, while remaining faithful to original biblical texts. Working closely with Botts, Sooy would create a font to support that goal.

Well Versed

As an active member of his local congregation, Sooy drew on his years of experience reading and observing readers of the Bible. Sooy had also designed the type family Veritas, which had been used for other editions of the Bible. He set to work creating a typeface that would work specifically for Tyndale's readers. He named it Lucerna, the Latin word for "lamp," based on a verse from The Book of Psalms. Lucerna's design is loosely based on Veritas, though the final result bears no resemblance.

The project goals outlined a strong, easy-to-read font that would work in a condensed format to dramatically reduce character count. At first, these requirements seemed mutually exclusive. Aesthetically influenced by the client's desire to retain the warmth of ITC Giovanni, used by Tyndale for typesetting earlier editions, Sooy studied its attributes in addition to those of Veritas. With those as reference points, and steady feedback from Botts, he applied himself vigorously to solving the problem.

Tyndale had previously used Giovanni for their publications, but needed a font that would allow them to increase the character count on each page. Sooy made side-by-side comparisons with Giovanni and other typefaces popular in religious publishing to assess his font's legibility, readability, and size.

A	A	d	d
J	J	e	e
K	K	f	f
M	M	s	s
N	N	t	t
U	U	h	h
R	R	y	y

Tyndale Book | Giovanni Book | Tyndale Book | Giovanni Book

hamburgerfonts
Berkeley Medium

hamburgerfonts
Giovanni

hamburgerfonts
Tyndale Book

hamburgerfonts
Weidemann Medium

Sooy removed serifs from some of the letterforms and used shorter serifs on others. He moderately constricted the horizontal scale, and increased the weight of vertical strokes to maximize contrast with curved lines. He carefully enlarged counters. Sooy made frequent comparisons with the fonts he was referencing, checking Lucerna for legibility and readability, and comparing word lengths. The resulting type family has strong, clean lines. It's compact, but distinctive, and meets the challenging technical and aesthetic requirements set forth in the project brief.

Spreading the Word, Stretching the Dollar
The design's success lies in its effectiveness. With a focus always on the message, Lucerna enhances the reading experience. Sooy says his design prevents reader distraction due to "illegibility, low contrast, unusual letterforms," while "drawing attention to the author of scripture and not the medium in which it is delivered." On a secular note, using Lucerna has saved money. Tyndale House reported a significant reduction in production costs. The publisher has realized a 10 percent saving on paper for each Bible printed (up to 1.5 million are printed each year), all the while increasing study-guide content by as much as 20 percent.

LUCERNA

Lucerna was commissioned by Tyndale House Publishers for the New Living Translation 2 (NLT2) Bible released in June 2004. An exclusive design in Roman, Italic, Bold, Bold Italic and Small Caps.

ABCDEFGHIJKLM
NOPQRSTUVWYXZ
abcdefghijklmnopqrs
tuvwxyz0123456789

**ABCDEFGHIJKLM
NOPQRSTUVWYXZ
abcdefghijklmnopqrs
tuvwxyz0123456789**

*ABCDEFGHIJKLM
NOPQRSTUVWYXZ
abcdefghijklmnopqrs
tuvwxyz0123456789*

*ABCDEFGHIJKLM
NOPQRSTUVWYXZ
abcdefghijklmnopqrst
uvwxyz0123456789*

Creating highly readable text fonts, in particular for Bible readers and of course publications has been my passion for many years. It's my firm conviction that readers of the world's most-read book should not be hindered by the font that is used to typeset it.

The initial considerations were:
• Better character count
  (to maximize space and ultimately save paper)
• Achieve better readability
• Eliminate artificial condensing of standard fonts
• Make the font "stronger"

The font is a design solution to these technical and aesthetic considerations. Its core design is based on Veritas (Altered Ego Fonts).

The name *Lucerna* is Latin for lamp, and is inspired by Psalms 119:105 – "Your word is a lamp for my feet and a light for my path." Seemed like the perfect name for a Bible translation that illuminates the Word of God.

ABCDEFGHIJKLM
NOPQRSTUVWYXZ
ABCDEFGHIJKLM
NOPQRSTUVWYXZ

ABCDEFGHIJKLM
NOPQRSTUVWYXZ
ABCDEFGHIJKLM
NOPQRSTUVWYXZ

Designed by Brian Sooy
www.AlteredEgoFonts.com

Sample page from The New Living Translation Bible:

page 21... GENESIS 21

The Birth of Isaac
21 Then the Lord did exactly what he had promised. 2Sarah became pregnant, and she gave a son to Abraham in his old age. It all happened at the time God had said it would. 3And Abraham named his son Isaac.* 4Eight days after Isaac was born, Abraham circumcised him as God had commanded. 5Abraham was one hundred years old at the time.
6And Sarah declared, "God has brought me laughter! All who hear about this will laugh with me. 7For who would have dreamed that I would ever have a baby? Yet I have given Abraham a son in his old age!"

Hagar and Ishmael Sent Away
8As time went by and Isaac grew and was weaned, Abraham gave a big party to celebrate the happy occasion. 9But Sarah saw Ishmael—the son of Abraham and her Egyptian servant Hagar—making fun of Isaac. 10So she turned to Abraham and demanded, "Get rid of that servant and her son. He is not going to share the family inheritance with my son, Isaac. I won't have it!"
11This upset Abraham very much because Ishmael was his son. 12But God told Abraham, "Do not be upset over the boy and your servant wife. Do just as Sarah says, for Isaac is the son through whom your descendants will be counted. 13But I will make a nation of the descendants of Hagar's son because he also is your son."
14So Abraham got up early the next morning, prepared food for the journey, and strapped a container of water to Hagar's shoulders. He sent her away with their son, and she walked out into the wilderness of Beersheba, wandering aimlessly. 15When the water was gone, she left the boy in the shade of a bush. 16Then she went and sat down by herself about a hundred yards* away. "I don't want to watch the boy die," she said, as she burst into tears.
17Then God heard the boy's cries, and the angel of God called to Hagar from the sky, "Hagar, what's wrong? Do not be afraid! God has heard the boy's cries from the place where you laid him. 18Go to him and comfort him, for I will make a great nation from his descendants."

21:16 Hebrew a bowshot.

19Then God opened Hagar's eyes, and she saw a well. She immediately filled her water container and gave the boy a drink. 20And God was with the boy as he grew up in the wilderness of Paran. He became an expert archer, 21and his mother arranged a marriage for him with a young woman from Egypt.

A Treaty with Abimelech
22About this time, Abimelech came with Phicol, his army commander, to visit Abraham. "It is clear that God helps you in everything you do," Abimelech said. 23"Swear to me in God's name that you won't deceive me, my children, or my grandchildren. I have been loyal to you, so now swear that you will be loyal to me and to this country in which you are living."
24Abraham replied, "All right, I swear to it!" 25Then Abraham complained to Abimelech about a well that Abimelech's servants had taken violently from Abraham's servants.
26"This is the first I've heard of it," Abimelech said. "And I have no idea who is responsible. Why didn't you say something about this before?" 27Then Abraham gave sheep and oxen to Abimelech, and they made a treaty. 28But when Abraham took seven additional ewe lambs and set them off by themselves, 29Abimelech asked, "Why are you doing that?"
30Abraham replied, "They are my gift to you as a public confirmation that I dug this well." 31So ever since, that place has been known as Beersheba—"well of the oath"—because that was where they had sworn an oath. 32After making their covenant, Abimelech left with Phicol, the commander of his army, and they returned home to the land of the Philistines. 33Then Abraham planted a tamarisk tree at Beersheba, and he worshiped the Lord, the Eternal God, at that place. 34And Abraham lived in Philistine country for a long time.

Abraham's Obedience Tested
22 Later on God tested Abraham's faith and obedience. "Abraham!" God called.
"Yes," he replied. "Here I am."
2"Take your son, your only son—yes, Isaac, whom you love so much—and go to the land of Moriah. Sacrifice him there as a burnt offer-

↑
Brian Sooy created Lucerna as a custom type family for Tyndale House Publishers. Designed for readability and economic practicality, it allowed for a 10 percent reduction in paper costs for Tyndale's New Living Translation Bible 2. With 1.5 million units produced each year, that's a significant saving.

The Lucerna specimen sheet is shown here.

Company

TesisDG

Design Team

José Neira,
Juan Pablo de
Gregorio,
Francisca Reyes,
Constanza Abbott

Client

Center for
Mathematical
Modeling (CMM),
Universidad
de Chile

Audience

Companies and
industries requiring
the services
of advanced
mathematical
analysis and
modeling, other
academics

A Numbers Game

Yelling the word "math" in a room crowded with designers might start a stampede for the exit.

This is not the case at TesisDG, a design studio that worked to promote the excellence and high level of expertise at the Center for Mathematical Modeling (CMM) at the University of Chile. The CMM was formed by a group of professors from the Department of Mathematical Engineering to work on commercial projects in need of applied mathematics. CMM provides custom analysis, algorithms, mathematical models, and software to businesses ranging from forestry and mining to aviation. Not losing sight of their academic roots, CMM is also a major research center with faculty and graduate students publishing papers about discrete mathematics, mathematical mechanics, randomness,

→

The project made extensive use of charts and graphs to illustrate the mathematical excellence of the center. This example showcases the number of times the center appears in academic publishing citations, placing the school in the top 100 applied mathematics programs worldwide.

information modeling, and many other topics. The center needed to communicate its world-class research capabilities to companies requiring advanced mathematical analysis and modeling, and to other like-minded academics who might become collaborators. Enter TesisDG, a boutique design firm in Santiago, Chile with a passion for numbers.

Visualizing Research

The CMM competes internationally as a cutting-edge research center. To address this international audience and compete with well-recognized names like Harvard, Oxford, and MIT, they needed marketing material that would make a statement. TesisDG chose an innovative approach by focusing on the math. Rather than creating a traditional college viewbook with images of the school, students, faculty, and surroundings, the team created an 80-page monograph, written in English, and illustrated by graphic diagrams dedicated to visualizing the intangible.

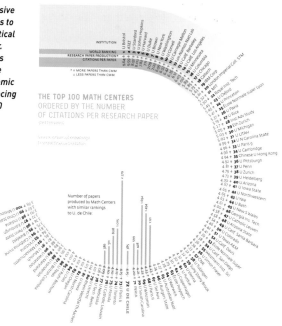

THE TOP 100 MATH CENTERS
ORDERED BY THE NUMBER
OF CITATIONS PER RESEARCH PAPER

Designers José Neira, Juan Pablo de Gregorio, Francisca Reyes, and Constanza Abbott collaborated on the job, working directly with mathematicians from the center. Open-minded and lucid thinkers, these professors generated mathematical models that would be used to create a series of illustrations alluding to the complexity, innovation, and abstract beauty of their science. Vibrant colors, flowing lines, and dynamic typography frame the theoretical graphics, which were then printed and artistically photographed to create dramatic perspectives of the two-dimensional work. Information graphics created specifically for the catalog visually define CMM's reputation for excellence, its broad array of services, and its client portfolio. These statistical displays and technical drawings have remarkably high information resolution. Select visualizations from prominent research projects were also used to provide direct examples of the center's work. This artfully balanced combination of complex imagery firmly supports the written content and provides a vivid illustration of the exciting and innovative work carried out at the center.

Solving the Equation

The catalog reinforces the center's reputation as an internationally recognized site of scientific excellence. By breaking with marketing convention and focusing on their client's core strengths, the design team produced a memorable document that visually positions the CMM in its rightful place as one of the top 100 mathematical centers in the world.

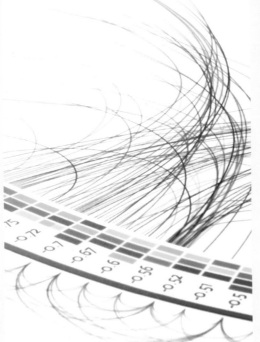

←↓
Technical drawings, based on mathematical models created by the Center for Mathematical Modeling faculty, were built digitally, printed, and photographed to create dramatic illustrations. These were used as section breaks throughout the monograph.

HistoryShots
Posters

Company

White Rhino

Design Team

Kimberly Cloutier
and Dan Greenwald
from White Rhino
and Larry Gormley
from HistoryShots

Client

HistoryShots

Audience

Historians, history
buffs, educators

The Art of Information Design

Presenting a vast amount of data in a compressed space is difficult to do effectively.

The designer must avoid clutter, emphasize critical points, and create something both useful and aesthetically pleasing. HistoryShots, a collection of infographic posters that present complex data through compelling visualization, exemplifies this bewildering challenge. Working with HistoryShots to create unique and engaging posters depicting historical events, the White Rhino designers have connected with the audience by providing clear and exciting designs that shed new light on major world events.

Designers Kimberly Cloutier and Dan Greenwald worked with Larry Gormley from HistoryShots to develop data visualizations that truly tell stories. Their posters seek to shed new light on history, using information design to retell familiar narratives. To be considered a success, the posters must be coveted for their content, yet attractive enough to appeal to someone who wants to hang them on the wall as art, because they are sold as high-quality prints.

Labor-intensive Design

Greenwald describes the poster-building process as a six- to nine-month affair, much of which is devoted to research. After the initial research, the designers create prototypes that help identify information gaps. As the editors work, the text is reduced to the absolute minimum required to tell the story. "This loop of data gathering, prototyping, and data reduction continues for many iterations before the design is finalized," says Greenwald. "Often the main issue is how to display the multi-variable data sets within an easy-to-follow and intriguing design." Although a considerable amount of data is culled from

the ultimate solution, much of the detail is used; not in the final graphic, but on the HistoryShots website for viewers who wish to learn more about the subject.

Creating beautiful and informative posters for this project proved challenging on many levels, Greenwald continues: "It is very difficult to show multi-variable data within two dimensions—for example, showing geographic movement over time." While always striving to create spectacular designs, White Rhino kept its focus on the goals of the client: "We spend a great deal of time trying to change the design to facilitate the story rather than trying to change the narrative to fit in a two-dimensional space." While the designer's role is critical and each print must be worthy of display, the content is what motivates the history buffs, educators, and others who make up the HistoryShots consumer base.

Small Space, Big Impact

Most of the posters are a standard 36 × 24in (91.4 × 61cm) size, but tell extremely complicated stories. The Race to the Moon graphic explains how the United States won the race to land the first person on the moon by illustrating the space programs of both the Soviet Union and the US, covering all manned missions up until the 1969 landing, and including details of launch vehicles, time in space, distance covered, and program costs. The Conquest of Everest poster uses concentric circles to chart the progress of climbers in 12 expeditions, from 1921 until the successful mission in 1953. Rather than solely concentrating on the well-worn tale of the latter, successful trip, the poster shows how each expedition contributed to the ultimate success of the 1953 team through the experience gained in planning and tactics. Perhaps White Rhino's most complicated poster designs are those demonstrating the History of the Confederate and Union Armies, respectively, during the 1861–1865 American

Civil War. These charts show the Union's victory by tracking the 23 Confederate armies and 31 Union armies in the various theaters of the Civil War—inspired by the famous statistical graphic of Napoleon's March to Moscow drawn by Charles Joseph Minard. Beyond the basic numbers, the posters demonstrate many variables, including history, commanding generals, and the name, location, date, casualty figures, and winners of the 100 most important battles. Viewers can track the effect of these factors on the successes and failures of each army.

The HistoryShots posters showcase the information designer's ability to paint a picture with data. "Our graphics look interesting and compelling from a distance, which in turn makes the viewer draw close and more deeply engage in the piece," says Greenwald. "The viewer can spend as much or as little time as they want interpreting the information."

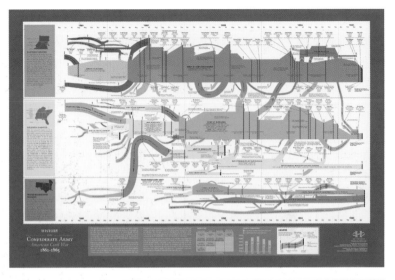

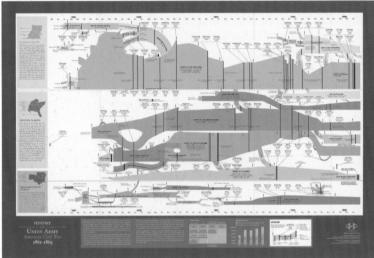

↗ ↗ →

Based on the Napoleon's March to Moscow graphic by Charles Joseph Minard, these posters track the Confederate and Union armies during the course of the Civil War. Each poster highlights troop movements, history, commanding generals, and

the name, location, date, casualty figures, and winners of the 100 most decisive engagements.

Detail of Union Army poster shown here.

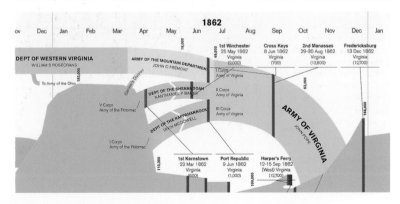

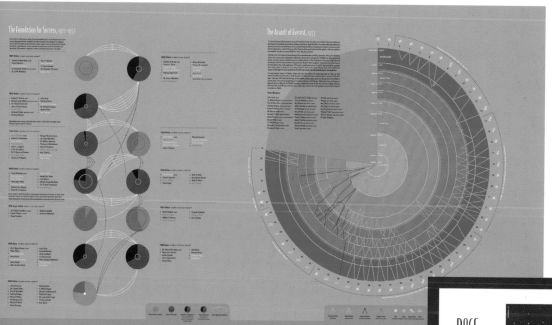

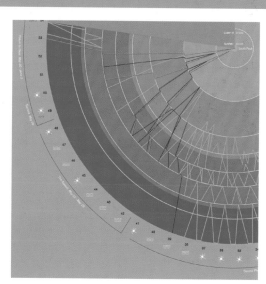

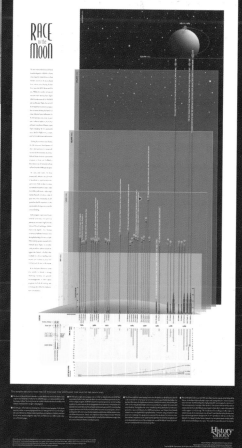

The Race to the Moon poster uses infographics to provide a very detailed account of the race to put a man on the moon. The poster includes details of time, astronauts, missions, vehicles, and cost, and provides supporting text to tell the full story of one of NASA's greatest achievements.

↑→
The Conquest of Everest poster tells the story of the 12 Everest expeditions leading up to the successful climb in 1953. A series of concentric rings, with the summit at the center, shows how close each expedition came to reaching the peak.

Glossary

A

ADA The Americans with Disabilities Act is legislation created to make American society accessible to people with disabilities. ADA design standard influences are numerous, from architecture to internet access to wayfinding.

AIDA A persuasive sales model, developed by E. St. Elmo Lewis, that describes the sales process as broken into four categories: Attention, Interest, Desire, and Action.

Ascender A stroke on a lowercase letter that rises above the meanline.

B

Baseline An imaginary line upon which type rests.

C

Cap Height is the measurement of the capital letters from the *baseline* to the top of the letterform.

Chunking Postulated by George Miller, a theory that the capacity for short-term memory varies among individuals, but that it is possible to measure it in "chunks." A chunk is any single unit of information. *See also: Miller's Magic Number*

Cleveland's Task Model A theory of perception, by William S. Cleveland, that has defined how we visually decode the content in graphic displays of statistical information. *See also: Pattern Perception* and *Table Lookup*

Columns Vertical areas on a grid used to contain text.

Counterform (sometimes simply referred to as a counter) is a negative space knocked out of a letterform. *See also: Form*

D

Descender A stroke on a lowercase letter that drops below the baseline.

Difference Threshold *See Weber's Law*

Display Font A decorative typeface, meant for limited use.

E

Em Web design measures type in ems—one em is equal to the point size of the font currently in use. Ems are a dynamic measurement, so when a user sets his or her on-screen size preferences, the type scales proportionally.

Eye Tracking is the study of where our gaze falls, and measures several different eye movements. Behavioral scientists and usability engineers divide these movements into *fixations, saccades,* and *scanpaths.*

F

Feedback is the response to a message, and can be categorized as direct or indirect.

Fixation occurs when our eyes appear to pause in a certain position. *See also: Eye Tracking*

Flow Line A common horizontal inclusion on the grid from which headlines, quotations, or body copy flow. Also known as a hanging line.

Focal Point The first thing that catches a viewer's eye when looking at a design piece, the focal point is the prime area of optical concentration.

Form refers to a positive shape, like the straight and curved lines (strokes) that make a letter. *See also: Counterform*

G

Gestalt Principles of Perception A theory by Gestalt psychologists which states that, in terms of visual perception, understanding is achieved by recognizing the interplay between design elements and concurrently reading the composition as a whole. Segments of this theory most relevant to the study of information design are the *Principle of Proximity*, the *Principle of Similarity*, the *Principle of Prägnanz*, and the *Principle of Closure*.

Grid Structural indications, comprising *margins*, *columns*, *gutters*, and *flow lines*, that create a framework for typographic and pictorial content.

Gutter On a grid, the space between columns of text. The term also refers to the interior margin of a spread, where binding can make part of the page difficult to read.

H

Hard Lead The first sentence or sometimes the first two sentences of a news story is considered a lead. Hard leads are concise statements that summarize the facts. *See also: Soft Lead*

Hierarchy In the context of graphic design, hierarchy refers to the ordering of pictorial and typographic information sets so that the viewer can quickly gain an understanding of their relative importance.

Human-centered Design *See User-centered Design*

I

Icons are semiotic signs that are also literal visual representations. *See also: Semiotics*

Inclusive Design *See Universal Design*

Indexes are semiotic signs that create connections between objects, using that which is easy to describe to identify something more obscure. *See also: Semiotics*

Information Literacy describes an individual's ability to recognize when information is needed, and then have the skills to find, evaluate, analyze, and effectively use that information.

Information Overload A term attributed to futurist Alvin Toffler, referring to an individual's inability to process, assimilate, and understand information due to the overwhelming amount of data available.

Interpersonal Communication focuses on interactions between a pair of individuals, or groups of individuals; it concerns the relationships between sender and receiver, message and feedback.

Inverted Pyramid Writing A common framework for journalism and online content, this writing style places the most important or newsworthy information at the beginning of the story, and orders the remaining information based on relative importance.

K

Kerning describes adjustments to the horizontal space between two individual letters. *See also: Tracking*

L

LATCH is a model for organizing information, developed by Richard Saul Wurman, that identifies just five ways to group content: Location, Alphabet, Time, Category, and Hierarchy.

Leading is sometimes called line spacing, and defines the vertical distance between lines of type (measured from baseline to baseline).

Learning Style A particular sensory method (or mode) of experiencing, interacting with, and remembering new information. The three most common learning styles are Visual, Auditory/Verbal, and Kinesthetic/Tactile. Visual learners prefer images when encountering new information. Verbal learners prefer experiencing new information in the form of written and spoken words. Kinesthetic learners acquire knowledge by doing.

Legibility refers to the traits that affect recognition of individual letters and words. *See also: Readability*

M

Margin The space around the edges of a page that defines a frame for content.

Mass Communication is concerned with relaying information to broader populations, and the effect of media on message.

Meanline The imaginary line above the baseline defined by the x-height of lowercase letters in any given typeface. *See also: X-height*

Miller's Magic Number An information-processing theory, by psychologist George Miller, which postulates that the human brain can remember seven chunks, plus or minus two, in short-term memory. *See also: Chunking*

P

Pattern Perception is a process that occurs when reading charts and graphs, during which viewers may be able to define a single trend or see migrations of data in different directions. *See also: Cleveland's Task Model*

Points In print design, type is measured in points (there are 72 points in an inch, or 28.35 points in a centimeter).

Principle of Closure states that we mentally close up or form objects that are visually implied. *See also: Gestalt Principles of Perception*

Principle of Least Effort This theory, by Thomas Mann, describes our natural proclivity to utilize tools that are simple, accessible, familiar, and comfortable. It states that ease of use may be more important to the researcher than the quality of results they find.

Principle of Prägnanz Also known as the figure–ground relationship, this principle states that when looking at a visual field, objects appear either dominant or recessive. *See also: Gestalt Principles of Perception*

Principle of Proximity states that when viewers see adjacent objects they process them as a group, and consider them to have like meaning. *See also: Gestalt Principles of Perception*

Principle of Similarity states that objects which share similar attributes—such as size, color, shape, direction, orientation, weight, and texture—are perceptually and cognitively grouped together. *See also: Gestalt Principles of Perception*

R

Rag The unaligned side of a text block that creates a more jagged shape.

Readability refers to the clarity and speed at which typographic content can be read in large quantities (paragraphs, pages, volumes).

Rivers of White When both sides of a text column are aligned (justified), the spacing of the text within becomes inconsistent, causing noticeable white spots to appear between words. This phenomenon negatively affects readability by distracting the viewer from the continuity of the text.

Route-based Knowledge When individuals use environmental cues and landmarks to choose their path. *See also: Wayfinding*

S

Saccade The movement between one fixation and the next—or the movement that occurs when the eye changes position. *See also: Eye Tracking*

Sans Serif Typeface design without serifs. *See also: Serif*

Scanpath is the term used to describe a series of fixations and saccades. *See also: Eye Tracking*

Semiotics is the study of signs and symbols as elements of language and communication. Semiotics strives to understand and explain how different meanings are assigned, based on variables of sender, receiver, context, and culture. *See also: Icons, Symbols,* and *Indexes*

Serif Typeface design with short, decorative lines extending from the strokes of the letterforms. *See also: Sans Serif*

Simultaneous Contrast describes color pairings that create a visual vibration when viewed together, and also combine to distort hue.

The effect is most intense when the colors paired are complementary and of the same approximate value.

Soft Lead The first sentence or sometimes the first two sentences of a news story is considered a lead. Soft leads take a more narrative or creative approach, setting a scene in which to place the facts. *See also: Hard Lead*

Stage Theory Model A widely accepted framework for understanding the process of memory that outlines the creation of memory in terms of notice, storage, and retrieval.

Strokes are the straight and curved lines that make a letterform.

Survey Knowledge When individuals look at representations of space, such as maps, to choose their path. *See also: Wayfinding*

Symbols are semiotic signs that are more abstract and may represent things that don't have physical form. *See also: Semiotics*

T

Table Lookup is a process that requires the reader to undertake a more detailed analysis of specific content in a chart or graph. *See also: Cleveland's Task Model*

Text Alignment Paragraphs or groupings of type can be aligned in several different ways. The axis point can be central, left, or right. Text can also be set so that both sides of the column are aligned, or justified.

Text Font A typeface designed for readability and versatility.

Tracking is the horizontal adjustment of space in a word, line, or paragraph of text. *See also: Kerning*

U

Uncertainty Reduction Theory An interpersonal communication principle that provides insight into social interaction, defining how individuals cope when meeting strangers. Developed by Berger and Calabrese.

Universal Design is a movement that focuses on clear, useful design that is accessible to everyone, regardless of age or physical ability. Universal Design artifacts are intended to appeal to a wide audience. The movement is rapidly taking hold in product, environmental, architectural, and software design fields, and can be applied to numerous other disciplines.

Usability Labs are facilities that test design artifacts, often digital media. Generally, users engage with the artifact while under observation. Feedback, gathered from a series of qualitative and quantitative tests, is used to determine a design's success.

User-centered Design puts the needs of people, the end users, first. Generally, this is an iterative development, incorporating user testing, feedback, and prototype revision to reach resolution.

V

Visual Literacy focuses on our ability to interpret, appreciate, gather, and create images. These images can aid thinking, clarify decision making, enhance learning, and strengthen communication.

W

Wayfinding describes how an individual orients him- or herself within a new environment, and the cognitive processes used to determine and follow a route, traversing from one point to the next. *See also: Survey Knowledge* and *Route-based Knowledge*

Weber's Law defines the minimum amount of change required, in any type of sensory stimulus, for an individual to take notice. That change is known as the *Difference Threshold*.

X

X-height describes the height of the main body of lowercase letters in a given typeface, measured by the height of the lower case "x," hence the name.

Contributors

Featured
Practitioners

**Adams + Associates
Design Consultants Inc.**
10 Morrow Avenue
Suite 101
Toronto, Ontario M6R 2J1
Canada
a-plus-a-design.com
(pp. 22, 135–137)

AdamsMorioka
8484 Wilshire Boulevard
Suite 600
Beverly Hills, CA 90211
USA
adamsmorioka.com
(pp. 22, 152–153)

C&G Partners
116 East 16th Street
10th Floor
New York, NY 10003
USA
cgpartnersllc.com
(pp. 22, 170–171)

Chopping Block
481 Broadway
3rd Floor
New York, NY 10013
USA
choppingblock.com
(pp. 22, 172–173)

Design Council
34 Bow Street
London WC2E 7DL
UK
designcouncil.org
(pp. 22, 174–175)

Drake Exhibits
1275 Main Street
Brewster, MA 02631
USA
drake-exhibits.com
(pp. 22, 176–177)

Eckes Design
601 Oakwood Drive
Anoka, MN 55303
USA
eckesdesign.com
(p. 98)

Enspace
18119 Detroit Road
Lakewood, OH 44107
USA
enspacedesign.com
(pp. 100, 119)

Explanation Graphics
205 South Compo Road
Westport, CT 06880
USA
nigelholmes.com
(pp. 22, 178–180)

Futurefarmers
499 Alabama Street
No. 114
San Francisco, CA 94110
USA
futurefarmers.com
(pp. 22, 181–183)

Glyphix Design Studio
Kent State University
213A Art Building
Kent, OH 44242
USA
kentglyphix.org
(p. 99)

Inaria
10 Plato Place
72–74 St. Dionis Road
London SW6 4TU
UK
inaria-design.com
(pp. 22, 184–185)

Jazz at Lincoln Center
33 West 60th Street
11th Floor
New York, NY 10023
USA
jalc.org
(pp. 22, 99, 186–187)

Justice Mapping Center
155 Washington Avenue
Brooklyn, NY 11205
USA
justicemapping.org
(pp. 22, 138–141)

Kick Design
347 Fifth Avenue
No. 1404
New York, NY 10016
USA
kickdesign.com
(pp. 22, 142–143)

**Andreas Koller &
Philipp Steinweber**
Austria
similardiversity.net
(pp. 22, 188–191)

**LACMTA Metro
Design Studio**
One Gateway Plaza
Los Angeles, CA 90012
USA
metro.net
(pp. 22, 144–145)

LA ink
2645 26th Avenue South
Minneapolis, MN 55406
USA
laink.com
(pp. 192–193)

Meeker & Associates, Inc.
56 Sherwood Drive
Larchmont, NY 10538
USA
meekerdesigns.com
(pp. 22, 154–155)

Nobel Web
Sturegatan 14
P.O. Box 5232
SE-102 45 Stockholm
Sweden
nobelprize.org
(pp. 22, 194–196)

Number 27
96 South Elliott Place
Studio 3
Brooklyn, NY 11217
USA
number27.org
p(pp. 22, 197–200)

Pentagram Design
204 Fifth Avenue
New York, NY 10010
USA
pentagram.com
(pp. 22, 70, 105–106,
146–148, 156–157)

**RDQLUS Design
Quantum**
7701 Pierce Street
No. 4
Omaha, NE 68124
USA
rdqlus.com
(p. 73)

Read Regular
Van der Lelijstraat 31
2614 ED Delft
The Netherlands
readregular.com
(pp. 22, 158–159)

Satellite Design
333 Bryant Street
No. 100
San Francisco, CA 94107
USA
satellite-design.com
(pp. 22, 160–161)

Scheme, LTD.
1215 Ramona Avenue
Lakewood, OH 44107
USA
schemestudio.com
(pp. 22, 162–163)

Small Design Firm
875 Massachusetts Avenue
Suite 11
Cambridge, MA 02139
USA
davidsmall.com
(pp. 108)

Sooy & Co.
151 Innovation Drive
Suite 220
Elyria, OH 44035
USA
sooyco.com
(pp. 201–202)

Spatial Information Design Lab
1172 Amsterdam Avenue
400 Avery Hall
Columbia University
New York, NY 10027
USA
spatialinformation designlab.org
(pp. 22, 138–141)

Stislow Design + Illustration
616 East 18th Street
Suite 4E
Brooklyn, NY 11226
USA
stislow.com
(p. 101)

Studio Panepinto, LLC
155 West Orchard Street
Allendale, NJ 07401
USA
studiopanepinto.com
(pp. 22, 164–165)

Sussman/Prejza & Company, Inc.
3525 Eastham Drive
Culver City, CA 90232
USA
sussmanprejza.com
(pp. 22, 149–150)

Terminal Design, Inc.
125 Congress Street
Brooklyn, NY 11201
USA
terminaldesign.com
(pp. 22, 154–155)

Tesis DG
Pasaje Lo Matta 1365
Vitacura, CP 765 0130,
Santiago
Chile
tesisdg.cl
(pp. 203–204)

Ultimate Symbol
31 Wilderness Drive
Stony Point, NY 10980
USA
ultimatesymbol.com
(pp. 22, 166–168)

White Rhino
41 Second Avenue
Burlington, MA 01803
USA
whiterhino.com
(pp. 205–207)

Contributors

Photo & Illustration Credits

Note: All charts, graphs, diagrams, and illustrations were created by the authors unless otherwise noted below. Ultimate Symbol's *Official Signs & Symbols 2* collection of digitized graphics was indispensable in that regard.

Chapter 1

IBM 360/75 computer image courtesy of the IBM Corporate Archive
(p. 10)

Chapter 2

Common Information Design Artifacts montage images on p. 22 also appear in case studies, Chapters 7–9.
(pp. 143-207)

Chapter 3

Ancestral Puebloan petroglyph image from istockphoto.com
(p. 28)

Maps influenced by Ptolemy's *Geographia* from superstock.com
(p. 31)

The iPhone is a trademark of Apple Inc.
(p. 32)

Google Maps™ mapping service is a trademark of Google
(p. 32)

Google Earth™ mapping service is a trademark of Google
(p. 32)

Willam Playfair's charts and graphs courtesy of Rare Book and Manuscript Library, University of Pennsylvania
(p. 33)

ISOTYPE images courtesy of the collection of Dr. Chris Mullen
(pp. 35-37)

Ladislav Sutnar images © Ladislav Sutnar, reproduced with the permission of the Ladislav Sutnar Family
(p. 39)

Mathematica, A World of Numbers and Beyond images courtesy of the IBM Corporate Archive
(pp. 41-43)

Pioneer Plaque image courtesy of the Johnson Space Center Digital Image Collection, NASA
(p. 45)

Visual Language Workshop images courtesy of and © MIT Media Lab. Financial Viewpoints mutual fund data in 3D, Lisa Strausfeld, VLW
(pp. 47-49)

Netscape browser is a trademark of Netscape Communications Corporation
(p. 50)

Chapter 4

Food pyramid images courtesy of the US Department of Agriculture
(pp. 56-57)

Colorado highway sign image from istockphoto.com
(p. 64)

Architect magazine spreads courtesy of Pentagram Design; Abbott Miller, Creative Director
(p. 70)

Back Roads & Beaches images courtesy of RDQLUS Design Quantum; Steve Gordon Jr., Designer
(p. 73)

Philips HeartStart Home Defibrillator images appear courtesy of Philips Healthcare, Royal Philips Electronics
(p. 76)

Chapter 5

Vietnam Memorial Wall image from istockphoto.com
(p. 83)

Handshake graphic from istockphoto.com
(p. 89)

Skull and crossbones images (top row and bottom left) from istockphoto.com
(p. 94)

Skull and crossbones images (bottom middle and right) courtesy of the authors
(p. 94)

Chapter 6

Circular grid image for MKE announcement courtesy of Eckes Design; Jodi Eckes, Designer (p. 98)

Environmental graphic for Kent State Athletics courtesy of Glyphix Design Studio; Amir Khosravi and Jerad Lavey, Designers (p. 99)

Images from jalc.org courtesy of JALC In-house Design; Daryl Long, Web Designer (p. 99)

Grid structure image from annual report courtesy of Enspace (p. 100)

Images of reichpaper. com courtesy of Stislow Design + Illustration (p. 101)

Dog and family images from istockphoto.com (p. 103)

Yale School of Forestry and Environmental Studies viewbook courtesy of Pentagram Design; Abbott Miller, Creative Director; James Shanks, Photography (pp. 105–106)

Nobel interactive wall display image courtesy of and © Small Design Firm, Inc. (p. 108)

Transportation signage image from istockphoto. com; color perception simulations generated by a free plug-in available at vischeck.com (p. 109)

Ishihara Color Test created by Dr. Shinobu Ishihara (p. 110)

Airport signage image from istockphoto.com (p. 111)

Safety color images from istockphoto.com (p. 113)

Bridal images from istockphoto.com (p. 114)

Chapter 7

Toronto Botanical Garden images courtesy of Adams + Associates (pp. 135–137)

Million Dollar Blocks images courtesy of JMC & SIDL (pp. 139–141)

Kickmap© images courtesy of Kick Design (p. 143)

Orange Line images courtesy of Metro Design Studio ©2008 LACMTA (p. 145)

Wall Street Rising interactive model images courtesy of Pentagram Design; Peter Mauss/ Esto Photography (pp. 147–148)

Roppongi Hills images courtesy of Sussman/ Prejza & Co., Inc. (p. 150)

Chapter 8

Marketing plan images courtesy of AdamsMorioka (p. 153)

ClearviewHwy images courtesy of Meeker & Associates and Terminal Design (pp. 154–155)

Sugar interface images courtesy of Pentagram Design. Laptop image courtesy of One Laptop Per Child (pp. 156–157)

Read Regular images courtesy of Read Regular (pp. 158–159)

The North Face instructional images courtesy of Satellite Design; Sandobox Studios, Photography (p. 161)

RiffWorks images courtesy of Scheme, LTD. (p. 163)

Mesü images courtesy of Studio Panepinto, LLC (pp. 164–165)

Official Signs and Icons 2 images and graphics courtesy of Ultimate Symbol (pp. 166–168)

Chapter 9

USPTO museum images courtesy of C&G Partners; David Sundberg/Esto Photography (p. 171)

MoMA What Is a Print? kiosk images courtesy of Chopping Block (p. 173)

Future Currents images courtesy of Design Council, © Design Council, 2006, Reproduced with permission (p. 175)

Demonstrative evidence images courtesy of Drake Exhibits (p. 177)

The Surplus and the Debt images courtesy of Explanation Graphics (p. 179)

Tour de Force infographic courtesy of Explanation Graphics (p. 180)

GOOD magazine infographics courtesy of Futurefarmers (pp. 182–183)

Xtreme Information brochure images courtesy of Inaria (p. 185)

JALC subscription campaign image courtesy of Jazz at Lincoln Center In-house Design (p. 187)

Similar Diversity images courtesy of Andreas Koller and Philipp Steinweber; Tobias Xaver Schererbauer, Photography (pp. 189–191)

Wall of Discovery images courtesy of LA ink (p. 193)

Interactive game images courtesy of Nobel Web (pp. 195–196)

We Feel Fine, Lovelines, and Wordcount images courtesy of Jonathan Harris (pp. 198–200)

Lucerna images courtesy of Sooy & Co. (pp. 201–202)

Center for Mathematical Modeling Catalog images courtesy of TesisDG (pp. 203–204)

HistoryShots images courtesy of HistoryShots and White Rhino (pp. 206–207)

AIGA | The professional association for design
http://www.aiga.org/

Communication Research Institute
http://www.communication.org.au/htdocs/

Design Council
http://designcouncil.org.uk/

InfoDesign: Understanding by Design
http://www.informationdesign.org/

The International Institute for Information Design
http://iiid.net/

International Organization for Standardization
http://www.iso.org/iso/

MIT Media Lab
http://www.media.mit.edu/

Society for Environmental Graphic Design
http://www.segd.org/

Society for Technical Communication
http://www.stc.org/

TED (Technology, Entertainment, Design) Ideas worth spreading
http://www.ted.com/

Usability Professionals' Association
http://www.upassoc.org/

Resources

Organizations & Websites

"694 Million People Currently Use the Internet Worldwide According To comScore Networks"

Press Release, 2006

http://www.comscore. com/press/release. asp?press=849

"Can You Tell Red from Green?"

Dr. Alex Wade, 2000

http://www.vischeck.com/ info/wade.php

"The Effects of Line Length on Reading Online News"

A. Dawn Shaikh, 2005, *Usability News*, vol. 7, issue 2

"The Effects of Line Length on Children and Adults' Online Reading Performance"

Michael Bernard, Marissa Fernandez, & Spring Hull, 2002 *Usability News*, vol. 4, issue 2

"Employment Outlook: 2003 Statistical Annex"
http://www.oecd.org

"End Nine-to-Five Working Day Says Sleep Council"

Press Release, 2001

http://www.sleepcouncil.com

"How Much Information? 2003"

Peter Lyman and Hal R. Varian, 2003

http://www2.sims.berkeley. edu/research/projects/how- much-info-2003/execsum. htm

"Information Design"

Sue Walker and Mark Barratt, 2007

http://designcouncil.org.uk/ en/About-Design/Design- Disciplines/Information- Design-by-Sue-Walker-and- Mark-Barratt/

"Information Design = Complexity + Interdisciplinarity + Experiment"

Gerlinde Schuller, 2007

http://www.aiga.org/ content.cfm/complexity- plus-interdisciplinarity- plus-experiment

"Information Design: What is it and Who Does it?"

Terry Irwin

aiga.org

"Information Interaction Design: A Unified Field Theory of Design"

Nathan Shedroff, 1994

nathan.com

Internet History Exhibit
http://www. computerhistory.org/ internet_history

"Longer Work Day Cutting Into Family Time: Study"

CBC News, 2007

cbc.ca, http://www.cbc.ca/ canada/story/2007/02/13/ family-time.html

"The Magical Number Seven, Plus or Minus Two: Some Limits on our Capacity for Processing Information"

by George A. Miller, *The Psychological Review*, 1956, vol. 63, pp. 81–97

"Muriel Cooper's Visible Wisdom"

Janet Abrams, 1994

http://aiga.org/content.cfm/ medalist-murielcooper

"One Day in America— America by the Numbers"

Nancy Gibbs, 2007

http://www.time.com/ time/specials/2007/ article/0,28804,1674995_ 1683300,00.html

"Richard Saul Wurman: The InfoDesign Interview"

Dirk Knemeyer, 2004

http://informationdesign. org/special/wurman_ interview.htm

"Shocked by Complexity: Q&A with Don Dansereau, PhD"

Cliff Atkinson

http://www.sociablemedia. com/articles_dansereau.htm

"Some Exploration in Initial Interaction and Beyond: Toward a Developmental Theory of Communication"

Charles Berger and Richard Calabrese, *Human Communication Research*, 1975, vol. 1, no. 2, pp. 99–112

"Typography and the Aging Eye: Typeface Legibility for Older Viewers with Vision Problems"

Paul Nini, 2006

http://www.aiga.org/ content.cfm/typography- and-the-aging-eye

Usage and Population Statistics
http://internetworldstats.com

"What is Information Design?"

Luigi Canali De Rossi, 2001

masterviews.com

Bibliography

Peter Barber
The Map Book
Walker & Company
2005

Rob Carter / John DeMao /
Sandy Wheeler
*Working with Type:
Exhibitions*
RotoVision
2000

William S. Cleveland
Visualizing Data
Hobart Press
1993

Sean Hall
*This Means This, This
Means That: A User's Guide
to Semiotics*
Laurence King
Publishers
2007

Robert Harris
*Information Graphics: A
Comprehensive Illustrated
Reference*
Oxford University Press
1999

Susan Hilligoss / Tharon
Howard
*Visual Communication: A
Writer's Guide, 2nd Edition*
Longman
2002

Mies Hora
Official Signs & Icons 2
Ultimate Symbol, Inc.
2005

Robert Jacobson
Information Design
MIT Press
2000

Iva Janákova-Knobloch
Ladislav Sutnar
Argo
2003

David Lewis-Williams
*The Mind in the Cave:
Consciousness and the
Origins of Art*
Thames & Hudson
2004

Ronnie Lipton
*The Practical Guide to
Information Design*
Wiley
2005

Knud Lönberg-Holm /
Ladislav Sutnar
*Catalog Design—New
Patterns in Product
Information*
Sweet's Catalog Service
1944

Kevin Lynch
The Image of the City
MIT Press
1960

Thomas Mann
*Library Research Models:
A Guide to Classification,
Cataloging, and Computers*
Oxford University
Press, USA
1993

Philip B. Meggs
*A History of Graphic
Design, 2nd Edition*
Van Nostrand Reinhold
1992

Eric Meyer
Designing Infographics
Hayden Books
1997

Paul Mijksenaar
*Visual Function:
An Introduction to
Information Design*
Princeton
Architectural Press
1997

Paul Mijksenaar /
Piet Westendorp
*Open Here: The Art of
Instructional Design*
Joost Elffers Books
1999

Josef Müller-Brockmann
*Grid Systems in Graphic
Design, Bilingual Edition*
Arthur Niggli
1996

John Neuhart / Marilyn
Neuhart
Eames Design
Harry N. Abrams
1989

Ian Noble / Russell Bestley
Visual Research
AVA Publishing
2004

William Playfair
*Playfair's Commercial
and Political Atlas and
Statistical Breviary*
Cambridge
University Press, UK
2005

John Rennie Short
*The World Through Maps:
A History of Cartography*
Firefly Books
2003

Erik Spiekermann /
E.M. Ginger
*Stop Stealing Sheep & Find
Out How Type Works*
Adobe Press
1993

Alvin Toffler
Future Shock
Bantam Books
1984

Edward R. Tufte
Envisioning Information
Graphics Press
1990

Edward R. Tufte
*The Visual Display of
Quantitative Information,
2nd Edition*
Graphics Press
2001

Edward R. Tufte
*Visual Explanations:
Images and Quantities,
Evidence and Narrative*
Graphics Press
1990

Richard Saul Wurman
Information Anxiety
Bantam Books
1990

Richard Saul Wurman
Information Anxiety 2
Que
2000

A

accessibility 144–5
Adams + Associates 135–7
AdamsMorioka 152–3
Admissions Marketing Plan
    152–3
AIDA 61, 77, 80–1
AIG Insurance Company
    176–7
AIGA 18, 21, 167
alignment 104, 129
Americans with Disabilities
    Act 111, 115, 117, 131
Andreessen, Marc 50
animations 173, 178–9
Arntz, Gerd 34
ARPANET 9–10
ascenders 122, 154
Atkinson and Shiffrin Model
    58–9
atmospheric conditions
    112–13, 115

B

Berger, Charles 88
Berners-Lee, Tim 50
Boston Edison
    Demonstrative
    Evidence 176–7
brackets 38–9, 60

C

C & G Partners 170–1
CAD modeling 176–7
Cailliau, Robert 50

Calabrese, Richard 88
cap height 122, 131
cave paintings 28
Center for Mathematical
    Modeling 203–4
CERN 50–1
character count 201–2
charts 33, 68–71, 152–3,
    206–7
Chopping Block 172–3
chunking 60–1, 74, 77
ClearviewHwy 154–5
Cleveland's Task Model
    68–70
cognition 60–1, 94
color
    casts 112
    coding 105, 107, 112,
    143, 145, 160–1, 188–91
    contrast 105, 112–13,
    115–17
    cultural associations 114
    environmental changes
    112–13, 115
    eyesight 108–11
    legibility 108–19
    perceptions 115
    structure 105, 107
    websites 115
columns 100, 104, 126
consistency 71, 101
context 14, 93–5
contrast 105, 112–13,
    115–19, 155
core content 105, 107

counterform 121, 154,
    158–9
culture 93, 95, 114
cuneiform script 29–30

D

data visualization 17
decision points 74
demonstrative evidence
    176–7
descenders 122
Design Council 21, 174–5
Designs of the time 174–5
difference thresholds
    62–3, 71
discernment 62–71
divided focus 12–13
Drake Exhibits 176–7
Dunn and Dunn Model 55–7
dyslexia 158–9

E

Eames, Charles and Ray
    40–3
Entry phase 88–9
environmental design
    112–13, 115, 149–50
ergonomics 25
ethnography 95, 144
evolutionary change 90
Excel spreadsheets 181–3
Exit phase 88–9
Explanation Graphics
    178–80
eye tracking 66–7, 71, 102
eyesight 108–11

F

familiarity 86–90, 104
Federal Highway
    Administration 154–5
Flash animations 173
Future Currents Campaign
    174–5
Future Shock 75
Futurefarmers 181–3

G

Gestalt Principles of
    Perception 64–5, 71
globalization 9–11
Golden Ratio 104
GOOD magazine 181–3
Google Earth 30, 32
graphical user interfaces
    156–7, 162–3
graphs 33, 68–71, 178–83,
    206–7
grayscale 103, 119
grids 71, 98–104, 142
grouping 98, 103

H

halation 154–5
Headstart 76
heat maps 67
hierarchies 80–3, 105–7,
    116–19, 131, 187
HistoryShots 205–7
Hockenberry, John 146
hue 115–17
human-centered design
    17, 25–6

human-computer
    interaction 25

I

icons 38–9, 93, 95, 166–8
Inaria Brand Design
    Consultants 184–5
Inclusive Design 111
indexes 93
infographics 180–3, 188–91
information
    anxiety 75
    bites 77
    density 23–4
    hierarchies 105–7
    literacy 91–2
    overload 75–7, 105
    volume 16
interactivity 40–3, 56–7,
    146–8, 171–3, 194–6
International Institute for
    Information Design 20
internet
    globalization 9, 11,
    14–15, 72
    see also websites
interpersonal
    communication 79, 81,
    88–90
Invent Now Studio 170–1
inverted pyramid writing
    84–5
Ishihara Color Test 110
ISO 13407 26
ISOTYPE 34–7
iterative design 25, 161

J

Jazz at Lincoln Center 186–7

journalism 84–5

just noticeable differences 62–3, 71

Justice Mapping Center 138–41

K

kerning 128

Kickmap 142–3

Koffka, Kurt 64

Köhler, Wolfgang 64

Koller, Andreas 188–91

L

LA Ink 192–3

language 9, 11, 95, 197–200

LATCH model 77, 82–3

leading 127

learning styles 55–7, 170

Least Effort Principle 61, 86–7

legibility 72, 77, 97, 108–31
  case studies 154–5, 158
  color 108–19
  contrast 105, 112–13, 115–19
  cultural associations 114
  environmental changes 112–13, 115
  eyesight 108–11
  typography 111, 120–31

Library of Congress 16

lighting conditions 112, 115

line length 126

literacy 61, 91–5, 156

Lönberg-Holm, Knud 38

London Climate Change Agency 174–5

Los Angeles County MTA 144–5

Lovelines 197–200

Low Carb Lane 175

Lucerna Type 201–2

Lynch, Kevin 72

M

MacNeil, Ronald 46

Manhattan Transportation Authority 167

Mann, Thomas 86–7

map shock 75, 105

MapMachine 30

maps 30–2, 72–4, 138–43

margins 100

marketing 67, 80–1, 152–3

Massachusetts Institute of Technology 46–9

Mathematica 40–3

media 14–15, 22–4

Meeker & Associates 154–5, 166

memory 58–61

Mesü Portion Control Bowls 164–5

Metro Design Studio 144–5

Metropolitan Transportation Authority 142–5

Miller's Magic Number 60–1, 74, 77

Million Dollar Blocks Maps 138–41

models 146–8, 176–7

Mori Building Company 149–50

motion graphics 171

movement 98, 102

Museum of Modern Art 172–3

N

NASA *Pioneer* Plaque 44–5

National Center for Supercomputing Applications 50

National Inventors Hall of Fame Foundation 170–1

navigation tools 156–7

Negroponte, Nicholas 46

Netscape Communications Corporation 50

Neurath, Otto 34

NeXT computers 50

Nobel Foundation 194–6

The North Face 160–1

Number 27 197–200

O

Occupational Safety and Health Administration 112

Official Signs & Icons 2 166–8

One Laptop Per Child 156–7

organization 80–5, 98–9, 101, 186

P

parentheses 38–9, 60

Patent and Trademark Office 170–1

pattern recognition 154–5

Pentagram Design 146–8, 156–7

perception 60–1, 62–71

Personal phase 88–9

petroglyphs 28

Philips Headstart 76

pictographs 29, 144–5, 156–7, 206–7

Pioneer Plaque 44–5

placement 103, 105, 107, 118

Playfair, William 33

Portion Control Bowls 164–5

proportions 104, 125

Ptolemy 30–1

R

Read Regular 158–9

readability 120, 125–9, 131, 154–5

reading disorders 158–9

Red Hat 156–7

revolutionary change 90

RiffWorks 162–3

Roppongi Hills 149–50

route-based knowledge 72

S

Sagan, Carl 44–5

Sagmeister, Stefan 188–91

Sanders, James 146

sans serif 111, 124, 130–1, 201–2

Satellite Design 160–1

satellite navigation 30, 32

saturation 115–17

scale models 146–8, 176–7

scanning 102, 142

Scheme, Ltd. 162–3

semiotics 93–5

serif 111, 124, 130–1, 201–2

signs 64–5, 73, 154–5, 166–8

Similar Diversity Infographic 188–91

simplicity 76–7

simultaneous contrast 115, 117

skimming 102, 142

Society for Environmental Graphic Designers 115, 136, 167

Sonoma Wire Works 162–3

Sooy & Co. 201–2

spacing 103, 107, 127–8

Spatial Information Design Lab 138–41

Spiekermann, Erik 125

Sports illustrated 180

spreadsheets 181–3

Stage Theory Model 58–9

Steinweber, Philipp 188–91

stroke width 123, 158

structure 38–9, 77, 97, 105–7
Studio Panepinto, LLC 164–5
Sugar GUI 156–7
The Surplus and the Debt 178–9
survey knowledge 72
Sussman/Prejza & Co., Inc. 149–50
Sutnar, Ladislav 38–9, 60
Sweet's Catalog 38–9
symbols 93, 95, 166–8

T
TED conference 82, 178–9
Terminal Design 154–5
TesisDG 203–4
texture 118
time 12–13, 82–3, 152–3
Toffler, Alvin 75
Toronto Botanical Garden 135–7
Tour de Force 180
tracking 128
trademarks 170–1
transparency 20
two-step technique 131
Tyndale House Publishers 201–2
typography
    case studies 154–5, 158–9, 181–3, 186, 201–2
    legibility 111, 120–31
    literacy 95
    maps 142

wayfinding 149–50
Weber's Law 62–3

U
Ultimate Symbol 166–8
Uncertainty Reduction Theory 88–90
Universal Design 111
University of Minnesota 192–3
University of Southern California 152–3
usability
    case studies 159
    grids 101
    testing 66, 71
    typography 125
user-centered design 17, 25–6

V
value (color) 115–17
Vietnam Memorial Wall 83
vischeck.com 108, 109
Visible Language Workshop 46–9
visual
    deficiencies 109
    hierarchies 105–7
    learners 55, 57
    literacy 91–2
visualization of data 17

W
Wall of Discovery 192–3
Wall Street Rising 146–8

wayfinding 72–4, 135–7, 144–5, 149–50, 166–8
We Feel Fine 197–200
Weber's Law 62–3, 71
websites 50–1
    case studies 172–3, 194–200
    color 115
    grids 104
Wertheimer, Max 64
What is a Print? 172–3
White Rhino 205–7
width-to-height ratio 123, 131
Wilson, Glenn 75
WordCount 197–200
working hours 12–13
World Wide Web Consortium 115
Wurman, Richard Saul 19, 75, 82–3

X
x-height 122, 125, 154
Xtreme Information 184–5

Z
Zipf, George 86–7

↓ Thanks

This book is a collaborative effort, and would not have been possible without the expertise of our contributors.

We are inspired by their work and honored by their participation.

Enspace Partner Craig Ihms helped shape the case-study section of the book. And thankfully, Partner Paul Perchinske is also a last-minute emergency photographer, vector-graphic guru, and design critic.

Mary Murray McDonald was an invaluable help gathering glossary terms, and Tom Humphrey excellent counsel regarding image rights.

Professor Paul Nini of OSU generously provided the sidebar information on page 111.

Lindy Dunlop, Tom Mugridge, April Sankey, and Tony Seddon have been excellent guides.

Our parents raised us on bedtime stories, piles of books, assorted art supplies, and a steady stream of expectation and encouragement. They were our first and remain our most influential role models. How do you thank someone for a lifetime of opportunity? (And now for hours and hours of unpaid babysitting?) We hope "We love you" will suffice.

And finally, thanks to our daughter Lulu, who has opened our eyes to new wonders and forced us to play every single day, deadlines be damned.

Jenn + Ken Visocky O'Grady are partners in business and life.

The couple cofounded Enspace, a creative think tank where collaboration enhances communication. The firm's work has been recognized by numerous organizations and featured in magazines and books. Together they have had the privilege to travel North America, jurying competitions and presenting workshops and lectures. They also promote the value of design in the classroom—Jenn as an Associate Professor at Cleveland State University, and Ken as an Assistant Professor at Kent State University.

Their first book, *A Designer's Research Manual*, is suggested preparatory text for a portion of the Canadian RGD Qualification Examination.

↑ About

The Authors